THE
MAGICAL
PLACE
WE CALL
School

THE
MAGICAL
PLACE
WE CALL
School

CREATING A SAFE SPACE FOR
LEARNING AND HAPPINESS
IN A CHALLENGING WORLD

Dr. Kathleen Corley
WITH GLENN PLASKIN

Forefront
BOOKS

Published by Forefront Books.
Distributed by Simon & Schuster.

Library of Congress Control Number: 2023916760

Print ISBN: 9781637632246
E-book ISBN: 9781637632253

Cover Design by George Stevens, G Sharp Design LLC
Interior Design by Bill Kersey, KerseyGraphics

This book is dedicated to my all-time favorite human—

my husband, the amazing Wayne Corley.

About the Cover

When I first saw Giuliano Giuggioli's painting of the Coliseum (*Il restauro*, *The Restoration*) in a high-end gallery in San Francisco, I was transfixed. While I remember very little about what else was on display in the gallery, I vividly recall my feelings when I stood in front of this one—it was one of the most impactful pieces of art I had ever seen. Then it became even more fascinating when the gallery attendant told me the artist's story.

Giuggioli's earlier works were primarily dark, serious-themed pieces; clearly not ones that I would be drawn to in any way. But then the artist and his wife had a baby, and he began to see the world through his child's eyes. That's when he added the colorful children's blocks—a sign of new life, energy, and exciting possibilities.

The reason I chose this painting of the Coliseum for my book cover, beyond the fact that it became a surprise gift from my husband, is that it has a similar meaning to me. Rebuilding the ruins of an ancient monument with children's blocks is, in a way, what teachers, administrators, and parents do every day. We teach children to appreciate the wonder and beauty of the world as it is, but we also empower them with the skills they need to make it better and brighter. The use of brightly colored blocks to "renovate" the Coliseum imparts a feeling of optimism and hope for our children's futures. It is that belief that makes school, when done right, "magical."

Contents

Preface

Stew's On

EVERY DECEMBER, JUST BEFORE THE HOLIDAY BREAK, OUR entire community of six hundred students at Red Cedar Elementary School in Bluffton, South Carolina, collaborates on the tastiest project imaginable.

In between classes, we go into the kitchen to whip up a version of Brunswick stew—a Southern dish with a tomato base. Typically, the ingredients include spinach, root vegetables, chicken, corn, and a touch of cayenne pepper.

Why am I talking about stew? Believe it or not, it's one of the most effective community-building activities we engage in at Red Cedar. And the effort it entails is indicative of the lengths we are willing to go in order to sustain and fortify our school community. Whatever it takes.

It's a holiday tradition that emphasizes unity and brings together students from ages five to twelve, all motivated by a sense of common purpose and fun. The adults don't miss out either: teachers, administrative staff, and parents, among others, all pitch in to produce this massive batch of hearty goodness.

Let it be said, too, that we don't just open a can. Instead, our fifth-grade math students gleefully take on the task of adapting a family recipe that typically serves five people into a recipe that yields *seven hundred servings*. As one ten-year-old smoothly noted for the local TV station covering our event, "Since the original recipe serves five people, we multiply every ingredient by 140, which is 700 divided by 5."

Neither do we simply follow the ingredients list in a cookbook. Instead, we produce a customized blend—our very own Red Cedar Stew—with particular elements that consider the tastes of our student body. Indeed, because more than half of our enrollment is composed of Hispanic students, many from Central America and rural Mexico, we use spicy condiments at their request. Specifically, we incorporate lime juice, cilantro, cumin, calabaza, boniato, yucca, malanga, and plantain to create our signature soup. To complete the flavor profile, corn, potatoes, and chicken are added. This unique mixture is a metaphor for who we are as a student body—a wonderful blend of cultures and customs.

We spread out the work, assigning a different ingredient to each grade level. Students bring what they can, from a single potato to a can of tomatoes. (Full disclosure: we have never received exactly what we ask for from each student, so we supplement the student offerings with a last-minute run to the grocery store.)

Finally, armed and ready, we plunge into Chop Day, which we have gotten down to a science. A squad of dicers and peelers composed of moms and dads, staff members, local church volunteers, firefighters, and police officers cleans and cuts the herbs and vegetables. The most amazing aromas waft through the cavernous atrium of the school, drawing students like bees to honey.

Then Cook Day starts. Every year a local chef with superior culinary skills (who is nearly always a parent of one of our students) makes the roux and sautés the peppers and onions. When that is ready, he directs the loading of all the ingredients into the six Low Country boil pots that steam away over propane-fueled flames. The result is not just a huge amount of stew but also a sense of pride in our community, a feat that proves we can gather together, use our creativity, and celebrate the holidays as one.

In short, Stew Day is iconic. It offers a special break from the hard work of the classroom. After all, students spend seven hours a day learning new skills and subjects; their heads are exploding with information. The stew project allows them to decompress. They watch the preparations with sheer fascination. And they love asking questions and making suggestions as they eagerly await a delicious result.

During the chopping, which takes place in the atrium, the aromas are overwhelming, even spilling out to the adjacent areas of the school. While it is cooking, those of us close to those boiling pots can smell it outside the cafeteria doors, but the children cannot because it's not safe to let them close enough to do so; they certainly can smell the stew when it is being served to them. By getting children out of the classroom and into the (outdoor) kitchen, we create something that is more than the sum of its parts. We create a spirit that is essential to our students' well-being and social development. They feel better doing it. And so do I.

Driving home after the event, I take stock of the day: Whom did we help? Whom did we educate? Whom did we lift up? Whom did we make laugh? Whom did we coach? And what did *I* learn? All these questions are key to my mission as the school's principal. Being an educational administrator is a job that has never been as complicated as it is in today's pandemic-hampered world. Now more than ever, my prime concern is discovering what supports students and their teachers in every possible way, helping them feel comfortable taking the next steps in their learning and teaching.

And that's why I decided to write this book. Over the course of a forty-year career, I've learned that my job as an educator is not to manage, dictate, and assess. It is to facilitate, inspire, and lead. It's to set an example for the students and the adults in the building. It's also to create the space each person needs to be the best they can be.

As I always say, nothing wonderful happens in the principal's office. Rather, the magic happens in the classroom. Once a principal truly understands this, his or her overarching mission becomes clear: remove any and all impediments between good teachers and good teaching. It's as uncomplicated as that.

But I didn't say it was easy.

You will no doubt note in the pages ahead that Red Cedar is not a cookie-cutter school where the teachers are just going through the motions; it is a progressive elementary school where teachers inspire, motivate, and set clear boundaries within a warm, supportive atmosphere.

As I see it, a school principal is weighted with considerable responsibility: six hundred souls are under my care—seven hundred when you count the adults who ably share the responsibility of tending to the students. I feel determined to do the best I can for each of them. I'm also driven to meet and exceed the South Carolina Department of Education's nine standards by which the performance of school principals is evaluated: vision, instructional leadership, effective management, climate (advocating, nurturing, and sustaining a positive, equitable school climate), school-community relations, ethical behavior, interpersonal skills, staff development, and professional development.[1]

To even have a shot at meeting these standards (which should, above all, include instilling in children a love of learning), a principal must first and foremost be a decent human being. I view my job as that of chief inspirer, motivator, cheerleader, quality control manager, coach, procurement officer, and construction-cone remover all in one. A principal

[1]   See South Carolina State Board of Education, "Expanded Program for Assisting, Developing, and Evaluating Principal Performance (PADEPP)," April 12, 2022, https://ed.sc.gov/educators/school-and-district-administrators/principal-evaluation/program-for-assisting-developing-and-evaluating-principal-performance-guidelines-2022.

should be willing and able to support teachers and students in any way possible.

In fact, I don't consider anything beneath me when it comes to serving the school or student population, and I cringe at teachers and assistant principals who believe principalship is a high calling that shields them from getting their hands dirty.

One morning, for instance, when I was filling in as principal for about four months at another school, I discovered a burst water pipe in the boys' restroom. As the custodian went off to fetch a wet vac, I mopped the water, directing it toward the drain on the floor to keep it from flowing into the hallway. Effective principals do such things. They believe in *keeping it real.*

As you continue reading about my enduring fascination with education, why teaching has been central to my life, and how the role of principal has changed over the years, I hope you will find greater perspective on the challenges we face today and the many novel and constructive ways in which we are always rising to meet them.

My career spans four decades during which various educational theories have gone in and out of fashion—and I've lived through every permutation. When it comes to studying and implementing the best ways to educate children, I've seen it all. (In a way I kind of hope I have; in another, I hope to see even better ways to do what we do.)

As someone who grew up in the 1970s, I'll compare the old-fashioned "factory" model of learning to the 2023 model, which is vastly different from a one-size-fits-all approach. Yesteryear's rigid structure and even more rigid application of discipline have yielded to a revolutionary progression in our understanding of students' emotionality—what they need most and how they learn best. Make no mistake: I don't advocate a lack of discipline and personal responsibility. On the contrary, I could write anthems to those qualities.

It's just that in my view, teachers should be leading and inspiring rather than micromanaging and disciplining. (And teachers need the same latitude from the administration.) Communication and sensitivity are paramount. We must understand *why* children do what they do. If we want structure and discipline in the classroom, we must come up with a humanistic, nonpunitive approach that supports children rather than squashes them.

In order to assess the needs of any student, we often must have an understanding of what is going on *outside* the classroom—at home, with the student's family. Of course, there are many positive stories in that realm. But I'll also tell you about some of the startling things we've learned during our home visits, especially when we enter environments where children have fallen victim to the ills that often accompany poverty, from lack of supervision and inadequate nutrition to devastating whole-family struggles. No amount of discipline will heal the spirit of a child who continually lives in trauma.

I'll discuss the transformation of our school culture writ large, brought about by computers, cell phones, Internet connections, and social media. The seeds of mobile-device addiction are surely planted in these early years. The convenience and magic of computers have advantages as well as drawbacks. I'll share my opinion that it often feels as though children are growing up too fast, exposed to news and information they may not need or know how to appropriately process, feeling pressured to compete in a world that is purely image-focused. I'll also offer our best practices to the extent that schools can help mitigate this reality.

You'll read about teacher-parent relationships, in which open communication is critical to a student's performance. There are many funny and sometimes harrowing stories teachers hear during parent-teacher conferences. In addition, because schools must use what leverage they can to inspire children to reach their maximum potential, I'll tell you about various leverage techniques that work when it might seem like securing and retaining students' attention is a pipe dream. I'll also share with you a number of stories that reveal how important it is to match the right teacher to the job and how I work with groups of others to marshal our forces and create a team mentality.

I'll tackle the subject of bullying, a harmful behavior that can negatively affect a child for years. As we all know, bullies can be aggressive toward children whom they consider "different," whether because of their weight, mannerisms, a disability, or something else. We have to protect not only the targets of bullying but also educate the bullies, getting them to understand that what they're doing is wrong. We must look into their minds and hearts to find out why, because every bully does bully for a reason.

I'll also share the lighter side of life in an elementary school. I've always been a believer in the power of fun, and you'll see the ways in which I've turned my own sense of playfulness into an asset.

The finesse and skill required by teachers today are beyond anything that was required decades ago. Our staff members must be jacks of all trades—counselors, nurses, confessors, and safety experts, all rolled into one. They do everything from teaching children how to tie their shoes to giving them nutrition and fitness information and instructing them about patriotism—not to mention teaching them reading, writing, and arithmetic. School staff members conduct fire drills, active shooter drills, earthquake drills, and tornado drills. Oh, and my principal colleagues and I are all crowd control managers. We have certificates to prove we passed that course.[2]

Not least important, we also have to be sensitive to parents' politics, tiptoeing around hot-button issues and academic subjects that they may not want their children to learn about, such as the civil rights movement, equity in all of its forms, and various historical events. (Mind you, that

---

[2] We earned our certificates from Crowd Manager Training, a division of Fire Marshal Support Services LLC: https://crowdmanagers.com.

does *not* mean we don't teach those things; if it's part of the curriculum, we teach it. But we need to be cognizant of the fact that there might be potential fallout when we're simply doing our jobs.) As educators know, some parents want to scrutinize the curriculum and completely control what their children are learning. It's not easy to navigate those treacherous and controversial waters, where virulent conflicting opinions eddy and swirl.

You'll read some incredible turnaround stories—instances in which we've altered the destiny of a student by conveying the notion that we truly care, because we most certainly do. These stories just go to show that miracles happen. Students change as they mature. Talents develop in the most surprising way. It's joyful to watch a student grow in understanding. Indeed, the last chapter of the book is my love letter to teachers, expressing everything I feel about the miracles they perform.

In the end, that's what it's all about. Caring. Nurturing. Listening. Observing. Teaching. And protecting children, especially in a world where school shootings are too common and where the weight of the world falls on children's shoulders—even the tiniest of shoulders. I don't think those shoulders were meant to carry the burden of adults' fallacies, biases, and mistakes.

Most important, I want to leave you with my vision for the ways in which education can mold minds, teach values, and create the potential for productive careers and happy homes. In that sense, we teachers and principals are the parents of hundreds of children. We spend a lot of time together, much like a family, as we help them learn about the world. That's our true mission, and it's a wonderful calling.

I'm very much an optimist. When my golf ball lands behind the trees, I'm far more likely to take the low-percentage shot through them than take a drop or go around. While I'm often successful, my skill level in golf doesn't always support those kinds of decisions on the links. However, I do carry that same anything-is-possible vibe into instructional leadership.

I must. No matter how slim the odds, my team and I are going to make positive things happen for our students and their families.

As a side note, I offer my lifelong support of the Chicago Cubs. The same optimism that keeps me cheering for them leads me to seek out staff members who are not only fellow underdog supporters but also excellent educators. What are the odds of finding those two traits together? Fairly high, I'd say, speaking from experience.

I hope that something in these stories from the front lines will resonate with educators, teachers, parents, and anyone else who believes that education is one of the most precious gifts we can give. Like the top chefs and sous-chefs in the very best restaurant kitchens, our teachers and administrators are worthy of "Michelin" stars for education. Beyond helping the community make the humble ingredients in Red Cedar Stew taste sublime one day a year, they work in unison the rest of the school year to foster joy in the classroom, elevate our students' experiences, and make a veritable feast of learning.

Our goal is always to make great things happen for children, even when obstacles exist and the odds are seemingly stacked against them. Some say that those odds cannot be overcome. I say, what do *they* know, anyway?

PART ONE

Building Bridges

CHAPTER 1

Seeking and Knowing

Every Child Has a Backstory

THE FIRST DAY OF SCHOOL.

Parents, as usual, arrive early and wait in the parking lot with their children for the 7:15 a.m. "Call to the Post" to play over the loudspeaker. These notes signal that it's time to enter the school.

At 7:40 a.m., a second musical selection sounds. (Traditional bells are so ordinary.) This one alerts the students that it is time to go to their classrooms. Then a third series of notes follows at 7:45 a.m., telling everyone that it is time for class to begin.

We have programmed our PA system to play a clip of Aretha Franklin's "Respect" at this final "bell" of the morning, not only to inspire and energize the students but also to send them the not-so-subtle message that they should treat one another and their teachers with *respect*. (RESPECT is our acronym for responsibility, empathy, self-discipline, positivity, effort, cooperation, and trustworthiness.)

By that time, around six hundred students have gleefully bounded into the school. Imagine the congestion of that crowd. If a drone were capturing the picture from above, the procession of little people would look like an orderly line of ants heading toward an apple pie on a picnic blanket! I love seeing all the new shoes, clean uniforms, bows on the heads of the littlest girls, fresh haircuts, and smiles for miles, all on display.

Most of the students would have already met their teachers the Friday before at a drop-in event, whereas others might have attended a "reveal" of classes the previous spring we call Taco-palooza—a warm-up for the following fall intended to build enthusiasm. Many have attended both events, increasing their anticipation for this day.

Even as a longtime principal, I'm nonetheless struck by how elated the students seem to be on the first day of school. They are happy to be together again—friends from different parts of town, for example, can see one another once more after a hiatus of several months. Most of the students' parents are happy as well, delighted to see their children reunited with friends and perhaps somewhat relieved to have them out of the house. And, of course, I cannot over-state the collective energy of the teachers and support staff who have been waiting anxiously for this day to arrive.

But I'm always touched by the kindergarteners' parents, who are often quite nervous about saying goodbye to their little ones. It can be heart-wrenching to watch. Sometimes at the parting, the child cries. The parents often cry, too, trying to hide their tears from their children and encourage bravery—their own as well as their children's.

To smooth the handover on that first day, and perhaps on just a few after that, many of the parents walk into class to get the four- and five-year-olds comfortable with the school environment, assuring them that there are no monsters lurking in the corners of our giant hallways.

While helping their children find their seats at one of our bright, primary-colored tables, which are perfectly coordinated with the room's walls, the parents also check out the toys and the cubbies where clothing is stored. Amid it all, the parents take lots of photos, making indelible memories of a landmark day in the lives of their children.

Meanwhile, our staff welcomes each parent one by one, assuring them that their children are going to have a spectacular first day. In short, we do everything we can to make this welcome back run smoothly.

And I must say that the youngest of our students adjust remarkably well. It isn't long before most of "the littles," as we call them, scramble into the classrooms, eager to engage with playthings and other novelties, while the older students cheerfully reunite with their teachers.

As for me, on that first morning of school, I am always in my usual spot for the 7:15 a.m. "Call to the Post." I'm perched on the sidewalk just in front of the main entrance, playing a musical instrument, as if I were the Pied Piper. (I'm a former music teacher whose uncle owned a music store, so I'm facile on several instruments.) My choice one year was a flute. I didn't play anything raucous—just jazzy, soothing riffs that I improvised on the spot. I know, as do most parents, I think, that I don't need to be all that good on the ukulele or the sax or whatever I grab. I just need to share something that fits the event. Whether I'm playing at arrivals or departures, or some other school experience, I want students to ask me how I do it, because then I can offer answers such as, "I learned the same way you do—a little bit at a time. And I practice."

Each day as I play, my eyes are focused on the children getting out of the cars, making sure, along with everyone else assigned to the task, that the ritual proceeds safely. I'm quite aware of the dangers of parents driving while juggling their cell phones and children hopping out of their cars. On rare occasions, a shy or fearful child will refuse to leave the car at all, and a battle of entreaties may ensue. It's a three-ring circus, to be sure, but a safe one because everyone we can put out there, including and especially our school resource officer, diligently supervises this arrival process.

A sense of euphoria is often present on this first day. This was especially true as students returned for the 2022–23 school year. After the chaos COVID-19 had caused for the previous two years, everyone craved a sense of normalcy. In retrospect, perhaps we all took for granted the freedoms we had before that awful virus staked its claim on our lives.

Fortunately, as you're reading these words, a large degree of normalcy has returned to school life. Our halls are filled with laughter, show-and-tell items, and fellowship, along with the sheer joy of some practical jokes. But of course, as they say, "stuff happens," and we have to be ready for *anything*—which leads me to the topic of how children behave in school, no matter what the season.

Matthew's Story [3]

Over the course of a long career, I've witnessed almost every variation of good (and not so good) child and adult behavior. And through it all, I often ask myself, *Now, why would a child* do *that?*

It's the *whys* that are intriguing to me. I tend to be both intuitive and analytical, and I never settle for a surface understanding of a child's behavior. Knowing the reason makes all the difference in how we approach the situation. Let me give you an example of what happened when I started out as a principal.

Matthew was a second grader who came to our school well after the academic year had begun. On his first morning, when he arrived by bus, I nodded at him and said, "Good morning." A moment later, I was shocked when he pushed another second grader right in front of that bus just as the driver disengaged the parking brake.

The other child, Mark, wasn't physically injured. But he was breathless with shock, clearly traumatized as we helped him to his feet. "Why did he do that?" the seven-year-old gasped. "I didn't do nothing to him."

Up until then, I had never seen a child wear a look of such sheer terror. The driver and I were just as frightened by the thought of what *could* have happened. In fact, had it not been for that very attentive bus

---

[3] The names of all the students and families in this book have been changed. The teachers' names, however, are their real ones.

driver and his quick reflexes, the morning would have been disastrous, and more than a few lives would have been forever changed.

In contrast to the panic I felt, Matthew's emotional state was calm as it could be. He had the face of a poker player. Nothing in his eyes gave any hint of what had just happened.

When I took him aside to talk with him, I was met with a vacant stare. I gleaned virtually nothing about his possible motive. While attempting to draw him out, he was only marginally communicative.

As I would later find out, Matthew felt like an outsider—disoriented, afraid, and alone. He had been bounced around from school to school. Ours was his third in just one year, his *fifth* since first grade. That troubling information certainly sent up red flags, even for me—a rookie principal who had been in that role for only three months before the event.

I told myself that children are resilient. They can handle a move or two and bounce back. They adjust. But that is not always the case, especially if they've reached a saturation point.

After further probing, it was clear to me that Matthew was quite angry about the many moves he had been forced to make. He had so much inner turmoil, he was like a bomb ready to explode. And on that day, he was feeling quite triggered.

After some tears and a face-to-face apology to his victim, Matthew opened up and explained his situation at home. He told me that when his parents moved him from his first school to his second, they promised to let him keep in touch with his old friends. But they had not done that. By the time he reached the third school, feeling alone as he did, he no longer bothered to ask his parents to maintain the connections. Instead, in a poignant admission, he confessed that his plan was to "do something really mean" to someone in his class. The reason? "So nobody will be my friend, and I won't miss anybody when I leave."

Instead of working to *make* friends at his new school, Matthew consciously engineered a way *not* to make friends at all. He went to that extreme to send a message to his parents.

Shortly after I finished talking with Matthew, I sent him into a small room by himself where he was still within my sight and earshot. I wanted him to reflect on his actions. I then reached out to his parents, who first declined my request for a conference at the school. But they did come in the following day. They described Matthew as a generally passive, quiet, but difficult child who was certainly not physically aggressive.

As his mom said, "He wouldn't consider hurting anyone. We can't understand why he would do something like this. It's just not like him."

I conveyed my thoughts about how difficult it is for children to be displaced from one school to another and how that displacement can result in acting-out behaviors. I also mentioned that while a child may seem passive at home, he or she may behave quite differently at school.

We then talked about Matthew's statement regarding his parents' promise to let him stay in contact with his friends. Exchanging glances with each other, the parents then minimized the importance of Matthew's connections to his former classmates. "I don't think he cares about that," his mother said. "And we don't have time for that kind of thing."

As I look back on it now, I know I didn't ask Matthew's parents the right questions. If I had the chance to do it over again, I would have asked,

- Don't you worry about your son's mental state?
- Do you wonder if he feels alone as a result of all the moves?
- Did you keep him in the loop regarding your plans?
- How would you feel in his situation?
- Have you connected Matthew with other families in the neighborhood or inquired about youth sports organizations in order to create a new life for him here?
- Would you reconsider helping him connect with his friends from his former schools so he might perceive his many moves as a

benefit rather than a disadvantage—one where he gets to have friends in many places, not just one?

I believe I knew the answers to those questions without asking them. But a more senior principal would have asked them anyway to get the parents thinking about what was best for Matthew.

In the years to come, my experience and research would prove one indisputable fact: a child must feel a strong sense of his or her place in the family, the school, and the community. And when that sense of belonging is shaken, the emotional ground beneath the child falls away. He parachutes into a new environment not knowing what to expect or what is expected of him. Nor does he know how long he might be a captive in his new world until it changes once again.

Matthew had every reason to believe that his stay at our school would not be long, so there was little point in getting chummy with anyone. He might have conducted a kind of emotional cost-benefit analysis on the price of isolation versus the cost of making friends whom he would soon leave behind. In this case, he chose the former. The result was a profound sense of loneliness and detachment from his peers.

Matthew's story is all too familiar. One of the most important tenets of early childhood education is the need to address the emotional needs of each child. If they're attended to, then the student is ready for what the teacher has planned for the day. But without the anchoring effect of emotional well-being, academic skills will suffer, and a child's concentration might be broken in one way or another. It is as if a child should be able to say to himself, even if he can't put it into words, *I am safe. I feel comfortable with the people around me, and I can interact positively with the other children in my class. I can predict what is going to happen throughout the day at home and at school.*

"Maslow before Bloom"

One fundamental tenet of education is known as "Maslow before Bloom," a phrase popular in academic circles. It refers to the work of the pioneering twentieth-century psychologists Abraham Maslow and Benjamin Bloom. The idea is that educators should meet students' basic needs for safety and belonging before turning to challenging academic tasks.

Bloom ranked the complexity of cognitive abilities from lowest to highest in his taxonomy of educational objectives. These abilities are *knowledge, comprehension, application, analysis, synthesis*, and *evaluation.* He believed a person develops intellectually through those levels, all the while building the capacity to grow in *knowledge, attitude*, and *skills*. In the fields of education and psychology, the knowledge and comprehension stages of Bloom's taxonomy has historically received the most attention.

Maslow's hierarchy of needs outlines five tiers of human requirements: *physiological needs, safety needs, love and belonging, esteem*, and *self-actualization*. It is easy to see that it would be nearly impossible for young children to function effectively in school without their physiological needs being met—food, water, shelter, clean air, sleep, exercise, and clothing, at the very least. But not every student arrives at our door with even *these* needs fulfilled. Beyond that, each student must have a sense of safety and stability. The third tier, belonging, includes friendship, family, community, and connection. Esteem includes confidence, recognition, achievement, and respect. The last tier, self-actualization, is something that occurs when all the other needs are met.

It's a tall order, to say the least. And you can see why "Maslow before Bloom" has become an educator's mantra. Sometimes we slip and forget this. And sometimes a good reminder is necessary.

Matthew's physical needs were being met, but his emotional needs were not. Worse, his parents did not realize it. I was so new to my job that I did little more than report this to them.

As threatening as Matthew's behavior was that day, he gave me a great gift—educating me about the ways in which loneliness and alienation can lead to aggressive behavior, even in a so-called passive child. Nowadays, whenever one of our students (especially one of the new ones) behaves aggressively to garner negative attention, I think back to Matthew. And I encourage our staff to ask the probing questions I should have asked Matthew's parents.

When it comes to new students arriving at our school, we do everything we can to offer a friendly, supportive environment, front-loading a sense of security for them so that they feel comfortable and welcome. Moreover, when we inevitably encounter students who are out of sync with the rhythm of an otherwise happy, positive, productive school culture, we know what to do.

Matthew taught me that we, as a school community, need to know about the history of each new student so that we can preemptively head off potential problems and ease the transition into our school. In other words, we have to know the journey all our students have traveled in order to understand the baggage they carry. Otherwise, we have no shot at understanding *them*. Put a different way, it's not enough to chastise students for poor behavior. You must know *why* they behave the way they do and address the antecedents of their actions.

Matthew almost certainly thought he was alone—that he was on an island, stranded, with nobody to care about him and no way of connecting with anyone. Unfortunately, as is often the case, his parents were oblivious to his feelings. Matthew's confession about purposely alienating students so he didn't have to suffer separation from them was, sadly, spot-on. On that first day, why *should* he have trusted anyone? We gave him little reason to do so.

Feeling alone is painful for adults. So imagine how devastating loneliness must be for little kids living in a world where everything seems overwhelmingly big. No child must ever feel that alone. And no adult should allow it to happen.

Digging Deep

My duty as a principal is to do everything I can to make children feel happy, competent, capable, and connected in the classroom so that they can perform at their maximum potential.

But this is obviously a tall order. Children are puzzles. Like all human beings, they are creatures of their moods. They can be friendly and approachable one moment and remote and detached the next. So as teachers and administrators, we have to be vigilant; we must be expert at reading verbal and nonverbal cues.

In a best-case scenario, a child really *wants* to come to school and do well. He or she feels energized and engaged in the classroom. But children don't always arrive at our door happy-go-lucky and ready to learn.

In fact, many come in moody or grumpy, distracted or sleepy. They might be wired up or down. When this is the case, we as teachers (and as one of their prime support systems) need to talk to them privately to better understand their states of mind. Doing some detective work about what's going on in their households can really help. Finding out the backstory often reveals why a student is late or why he's hungry, quiet, combative, yawning, or disengaged.

For example, our efforts can help reveal why one seven-year-old child's first impulse is to lash out verbally or physically at someone else; why a student is sitting with a glazed expression on his face, completely tuned out, as though he is alone on a desert island; or why a child is failing a class he used to do well in and enjoy.

Is there trauma in that child's home? Is there neglect or abuse? Is he simply staying up late in an attempt to become a junior Instagram influencer? There are countless possible reasons. We need to dig deep into the background stories of these children and examine their behaviors in order to meet their needs and help them be their best.

Max's Story

Max was a generally happy third grader, though not a tremendously studious little guy. His reading skills were the main challenge. And that's why his teachers worked overtime to keep him engaged and on a par with his peers, performing satisfactorily at grade level. But there were behavioral issues that inhibited his academic performance.

I had known Max's older brother, Nolan, because he had attended our school. By the time Max was having his issues, Nolan was in seventh grade. An extremely extroverted, assertive child, Nolan is quite intelligent and very social. Boy, could that child talk. He just never stopped.

As the school year neared its close, Max's name was coming up too frequently for making nasty, sexual, or just plain rude comments to another student. When confronted, he denied saying such things. Then he became upset that he was caught in a lie. After the third incident, our assistant principal, Cynthia, had a "Come on, man" moment with him.

"All right, Max," Cynthia said. "No more messing around. What is it with you? Why are you acting like this? This is not you. Or is it?"

After some pushback and deflection, the truth was revealed. Max had reached the limit of his tolerance toward Nolan, who had apparently been mercilessly picking on him. Max had packed up all those emotions, as well as the ugly, degrading words Nolan had learned in seventh grade, and brought them to school with him. What made matters worse was the fact that in South Carolina if a child fails the state's standardized reading skills test by a significant margin at the end of the third grade, the child can be prevented from moving on to the next grade level, with a few exceptions. Max was convinced he was going to fail that test and be held back. His reaction was to give up. And that is something we never want to see. (Spoiler alert: Max did fail, but not to the degree that would require him to repeat the third grade.) After spending some time talking things out with Max, Cynthia called his mom, and they made a plan to address the situation.

Max and Nolan's mom had always been cooperative with us concerning her sons. Despite her sincere intentions, however, the results were not always productive. Family matters, including unexpected deaths, and other significant challenges in her life overwhelmed her. So while Cynthia's "client" was Max in this scenario, she and the school also needed to serve Mom.

Mom agreed to meet with our counselor, our social worker, and Cynthia to see what could be done to help Max—and her, if she would allow it. If parents are willing, there are many ways we can and do assist them in managing the ever-changing and challenging world of parenting. Our motto is "Whatever it takes," and we mean it. Anything that will help parents support their children's success is on the table.

The team's plan for Max involved intensive academic support services, assistance from our counselor, summer school (along with an extra dose of fun to keep Max's interest), close follow-up from Cynthia, and a check-in system between the social worker and Mom. We carefully prepared Max's new teacher for the subsequent school year and monitored and adjusted Max's and Mom's plans as needed. Sometimes it does indeed take a village. Now into his fourth grade year, we have adjusted the plan to exclude some interventions no longer necessary and a check-in with Edwin Rodriguez, known as Eddie to the adults in the building and Mr. Rod to the students, our behavior management professional.

Reading the Signs

Trust me: there is *always* a reason for a student's acting-out behavior, and the most successful teachers and administrators know how to see beyond it to the truth.

Unlike the educational system of years past, in which administrators and teachers just steamrolled over students with rules and assignments, today's educational environment demands that we pick up on the clues that point to potential problems in children's inner lives. We can't ignore the warning signs of their disengaged behavior or just command them to do what we want them to do with little thought of how they're feeling.

Instead, we need to encourage the right behavior while continually striving to understand what's going on with them emotionally. This requires diagnosing the *whys* behind their behavior. How do we do this?

First, we use the powers of observation.

There is a vast difference between a child scowling, looking despondent, or slouching in his chair with his shoulders hunched and an exuberantly happy child with an open expression and an air of physical confidence.

The slouch, for instance, might suggest the child is tired, bored, or afraid. Maybe he got to bed late last night. Maybe he's hungry. Maybe he's unchallenged by his assignments. Or maybe he witnessed his mother being abused that morning. We need to find out the specifics because that child's mental state could be injurious to him.

Beyond the obvious signs of distress, there are subtle clues in facial expressions and body language. In fact, nonverbal communication is just as powerful as anything a child says. So we have to tune in to children's bandwidth and read their emotions through their bodies. Our teachers are expert at picking up these signs; some are incredibly intuitive about it.

We also remain alert to any potential medical problems.

Like doctors, teachers need to know exactly what we are treating before we can prescribe a remedy. A doctor, for example, might contemplate, *Is the patient with raging abdominal pains suffering from food poisoning? Or did he just eat too much sugar for breakfast?* The answer, of course, will dictate his course of action.

Sometimes, with parental consent, we need to evaluate a child for a possible learning disability. We might also need to collect data about a child's birth: Was he or she carried to full term? Were there any medical interventions just after the birth? When did the child reach certain milestones, such as crawling, walking, and talking? These determinations generally occur at prekindergarten screenings or when difficulties arise in a student's ability to perform well academically.

At other times, we need to call in experts to check basic functions such as a child's vision and hearing. More detailed evaluations can be conducted by a speech pathologist, psychologist, or social worker.

The bottom line is that as educators, we must *know* as much as possible to determine how we can help. And we must be *willing* to do so much more than just teach a particular curriculum and keep a semblance of order in the classroom. We need to dedicate ourselves to understanding the psyches and real-life conditions of all the students in our care. We must help *them* help themselves.

A Single Mother

The importance of understanding what's going on in a student's life outside of school was brought home to me yet again when I discovered that three siblings—one in elementary school, one in middle school, and one in high school—would often be absent from class. But each would be absent on a different day of the week, which was puzzling.

Then the staff and I remembered that these siblings had another sibling at home, a baby. We concluded, accurately, that the children were staying home from school to provide day care for the child while their mother, who was single, went to work.

The mom, Mrs. Grant, had no idea we would figure out what she was doing until we told her that we needed to meet with her regarding her children's attendance. In the meeting, after we described what was happening, Mrs. Grant's defenses broke down. She said she just didn't know what to do. She knew no one at the school or in her neighborhood who could care for her youngest; her parents lived three states away.

Fortunately, we were able to connect Mrs. Grant with another single mom in the neighborhood whose mother lived with the family. This grandmother agreed to care for Mrs. Grant's baby a few days a week. Mrs. Grant subsequently got her work schedule changed so that she could cover the rest of the days, eliminating the need for the older siblings to miss school. This was a brilliant resolution to the problem, one that would have been impossible without our knowledge of the family situation. Once the mom's big secret was out and we crafted a solution, her change in demeanor was striking. She even walked into parent-teacher conferences with greater confidence.

The intel on that siblings-as-babysitters arrangement was easy for me to suss out. My father was the youngest of five and significantly younger than his older siblings. His brothers and sister took turns caring for him until the truant officer caught them at it. With Mrs. Grant, I had a feeling that history was repeating itself.

Home Visits

Before COVID-19 made them virtually impossible, we conducted home visits. Understanding what is happening at a student's home is crucial to the efforts of teachers and administrators, which is why we make every effort to connect with families *before* the school year starts. Now, in the case of our prekindergartners, we form teams consisting of teachers, teaching assistants, and other professionals and conduct initial visits (usually by Zoom), which is so much better than meeting for the first time at school.

These can be very revealing for the teaching team because we get the opportunity to see students in the environment in which they are most comfortable. We can ask questions about their favorite toys, their preferred and nonpreferred activities, their playmates, their family relationships, the daily household routine, and more.

To accommodate non-English-speaking parents, we include a translator if the teacher who leads the group is not bilingual. On these virtual visits, we absorb everything that's going on, especially the mood of the household and the level of affection and/or tension. Everything that might affect the child's success at school is fodder for this visit.

The following are a few things we look for:

- What is the interplay between the child, his siblings, and other relatives living in the home?
- How long has the family lived in the area?
- What makes the child smile?
- How good is he or she at sharing?
- Is there evidence that kindness is valued in the home?
- How independent does the child seem to be?
- Are there any overt signs of potential special needs?
- Has the child had any previous school or day care experience?
- Are there signs of books or other reading materials in the home?
- Is the family in need of anything that we can supply?
- Does the family live in a multifamily or single-family dwelling?

After the teams conduct these visits, they are quite energized about what they've seen and better able to meet the students' needs.

CHAPTER 2
Applying Leverage

An Educator's Best Tool

TEACHERS ARE KNOWN FOR BEING RESOURCEFUL—FOR making something useful from the most meager materials. But there is one resource that has proven invaluable over the years: Whatever *leverage* you have in the classroom, I urge you to use it. Examples of leverage are the positive things you've done to successfully encourage students to listen to you, respect you, and strive to be the best versions of themselves they can manage to be. As long as it's not immoral, illegal, unkind, or inappropriate, I wholeheartedly encourage you to use these tools to make something good happen for students.

If you capitalize on the leverage you have, your students will feel motivated. They will behave well. You won't have to bribe or lecture them. They won't be tired, stressed, or frustrated. Used correctly, leverage can be so powerful that even the most difficult students will need no more than a glance from you to curb their disobedient behavior.

- One of my favorite articles about smart classroom management reveals the secrets of creating leverage to engage your students.[4] The author, Michael Linsin, lays out some wonderful tips.

- High on his list are *being likable* and *building a trusting rapport* with students. In my experience, these are essential. I believe that *sharing your gifts* with students is one way to do this. It strengthens your engagement with them. It forms connections with the children who have the same interests and talents, and for the others, it simply makes lessons more creative and fun. In this same vein, Linsin suggests *using humor and great storytelling.* I find that *making students feel safe* in any way you can eases the path to trust as well.

- *Having a clean, organized, and peaceful classroom* is on both of our lists. It helps children anticipate what is expected of them in the classroom and enables them to predict what will occur throughout the instructional day. It also assures that the tools they need will be easily accessible to them.

- What's more, Linsin recommends *setting challenging goals* for students, *following up with meaningful praise,* and *allowing freedom within boundaries.* These are among the day-to-day objectives.

- Among the big-picture ones, Linsin recommends *transforming your students' limiting beliefs about themselves; holding students accountable without causing resentment;* and *treating the causes of behavior problems, not the symptoms.* There are others, which you can find in the full article.

- To those I would add *allow no one to disturb the vibe in your classroom, including yourself; ask for help when you need it; expect the best from your students and yourself; evolve;* and *collaborate.* And, as stated in chapter 1, *understand each student's background story.* The more knowledge you have about a student, the more power you have to help him.

4   Michael Linsin, "Why You Need Leverage for Classroom Management...and How to Get It," *Smart Classroom Management,* https://smartclassroommanagement.com/2010/04/17/classroom-management-and-leverage.

The Pink Panther

My earliest professional encounter with the power of leverage occurred when I was a music teacher in Palatine, Illinois. My job was to help students develop an appreciation for the arts and teach them to sing and play instruments. I seemed to have a natural ability to hold students' attention, not allowing them to stray from the task at hand. But I often heard other teachers complain bitterly about students who were unruly and disrespectful. They couldn't control those students. It made me realize that they had no leverage and therefore were unable to maintain order. To be fair, an elementary classroom teacher might well be responsible for engaging the same students all day (including the least able or willing to attend to the rigors of learning). Related arts teachers, like I had been, generally have many classes to teach throughout the day, usually in thirty- or forty-minute increments. The challenges differ.

As teachers, though, all of us have the power to orchestrate what happens inside the walls of our classrooms. If, for example (giving away my age), you want your students to moonwalk out into the hall as they exit your classroom, it *is* possible to make that happen. But boundaries are key. In my case, I decided early on that no matter how ill-behaved students were when they arrived at the door, they would enter my room quietly and go to their assigned seats in an orderly fashion. They would also leave the room just as quietly once our time together was over. (In between this silent entry and exit, rest assured that we made plenty of raucous noise during the course of the class.)

To accomplish this Zen-like feat, I would sit at the piano playing Henry Mancini's theme from *The Pink Panther* as students entered the class. I informed each class (just once) that whenever they heard that music, they had to be quiet.

Why? Because the Pink Panther is silent—and that's his song, of course. This fact appealed to the children's imaginations. They loved it. And they more than complied with my directive, even smiling as they did so. Most took on the persona of the Pink Panther himself, crouching slightly, hanging their "paws" down at an angle at the wrist, creeping stealthily in and out of the music room.

We'd have great fun and learn some things during the period they were with me, but I could not send them back to their homeroom teachers all wound up and hanging from the ceiling.

That's what I call leverage—a creative strategy students genuinely like and one that helps maintain order in the classroom.

Since my days as a music teacher, I've often thought about how much leverage I had over the behavior of my students—how much influence I had over their attitudes. This, of course, had a direct effect on their ability to settle into the class and learn.

In fact, as my career developed and I went on to become principal at four different elementary schools, I used the theme from *The Pink Panther* as our "let's get ready to leave" song. I'd even play it in the cafeteria as students finished their lunches and got ready to go back to class. They would immediately sit up straight, make sure their tables were squared away, and sometimes pretend to *be* the panther, just as my students in music class did so many years earlier.

In addition to playing the piano for students, I lead the Foxes Rock Drum and Dance team—a group ranging from thirty to ninety students. Every Tuesday and Thursday at 7:15 a.m., we form a marching band with our dance teacher and our music teacher on bass drum. It's incredibly loud and great fun for all, to say the least. (My Apple Watch dutifully reminds me about five minutes in that we might want to lower the decibel level just a bit.) We participate in parades and sometimes accept invitations to put on special performances. This group has bolstered us all with a great sense of school pride, even when we're not perfect. It's the effort that counts. And no matter what happens, the students delight in the faces I make when everything comes together—as well as the ones I make when they do not. Using humor is always a plus.

Personal Touch and Positive Reinforcement

Another key to gaining leverage over children is getting to know them as people rather than seeing them as just another face in a group. Now that I'm a principal, it's difficult to do that, but when I can make that kind of personal connection, I do. Our assistant principal and I both receive emails that reinforce our belief that the personal touch makes all the difference. We also send emails to certain staff members along the lines of, "I was just informed that Maria has been trying so hard to improve her reading, and she just went up three levels! If you are anywhere near her today, please congratulate her." And as we mention countless times throughout the school year, "Students don't care how much you know until they know how much you care."

Many years ago, a teacher sent me a report about a student named Antwan, a stoic second grader who had struggled with math. But with the encouragement of his classroom teacher, the help of a math interventionist, and much effort on his part, he had mastered his math facts. I congratulated him for this feat and told him that he should be very proud.

Antwan's reaction was not what I expected. With a quizzical look, he asked me, "How do you know about my math facts?"

I explained that all kinds of people knew about his accomplishment, and it was a darn big deal.

He smiled shyly, asking, "Are they all as excited about it as you are?"

I assured him they were: "Maybe even more!"

He walked away, muttering, "Math facts. It's not like I went to the moon or anything."

But as Antwan learned, we celebrate milestones. And he got used to it. I can tell you that this kind of positive reinforcement is another mighty tool for gaining leverage.

Bryson's Story

One of my first experiences as principal at an elementary school in Bluffton, SC, involved dealing with a minor behavioral issue that caught my attention. Bryson, a fifth grader, was running in the hallway. I was in a spot where he couldn't see me. But when he rounded the bend and I came into view, he slowed down to a walk, believing this would trick me into thinking he was innocent.

"Hey," I said. "Why did you just do that?"

Quick to reply, he said, "I wasn't doin' nothing."

I hate that phrase for a couple of reasons, which became the gist of my conversation with him. "OK, here's the thing," I began. "First, let's take care of the grammar. I believe you're telling me that you were not doing *anything*. If that's the case, you'd say, 'I was doing nothing wrong' or 'I wasn't doing anything wrong.' Got that?"

He nodded in agreement.

"So you're saying that you weren't doing anything wrong, like running in the hallway?"

Another nod.

I went on. "Next, we have the issue of what I *saw* you doing. That would be running in the hallway. I'm pretty sure you weren't supposed to do that at your last school, and you likely know that you should not do it here. Is that accurate?"

He agreed.

This step-by-step gentle reasoning—another technique for gaining leverage—leads a child to understanding and thus to an inclination to comply with the rules.

"So why did you choose not to tell me the truth? Lying is the big deal here, not running in the hallway. There are zero consequences for running. But dishonesty is a whole other issue."

I proceeded to lay it on ever so thickly, because I knew that this fifth grader was going to spread the word to his pals about what kind of behavior I expected. After all, ten-year-old "influencers" have a very active face-to-face social network.

His punishment for lying? He was "sentenced" to writing a reflection about what he did instead of playing with his friends at recess. We reviewed it after he finished and talked about the lessons learned (likely more aspirational than real at that point). There were other misbehaviors that arose with Bryson, but our conversations about them were thereafter elevated to a more productive level each time they occurred.

Fast-forward several weeks: another fifth grader came bounding around the corner even faster than Bryson had. When the boy saw me, he slowed to a walk, just as Bryson did, in an attempt to feign innocence.

"Were you running in the hall?" I asked him.

He began to shake his head, but then Bryson intervened. "Dude!" he said. "Just tell her you were running, because we already saw that you were, and she really doesn't like that. And if you say it wrong, like with the wrong words, she doesn't like that either. And, like, don't lie."

I had to stifle a smile as Bryson's "mentee" grudgingly talked with me about running in the hallway.

From that point on, Bryson and I had a bond. Small though it was, it was a connection, built on that first moment. It meant something to us and provided me with leverage that led to some very positive things happening in Bryson's school life.

In short, however children present themselves to us, we as teachers and administrators need to build bridges in order to get them from where they are to where we need them to go.

Jeremy's Story

Consider the example of Jeremy, who started at our school as a kindergartner and was with us through fifth grade. He is a boy with more physical and emotional challenges than you can count on both hands. His mom also had some challenges before he was born. Shortly after Jeremy's birth, it was determined that he had three medical conditions that necessitated several surgeries. At some point, his parents split up. Thereafter, his overwhelmed mom concluded that she could no longer care for him, so she ceded custody to the boy's father. There were times when she promised to visit him or allow him to visit her, but she often canceled at the last minute, badly disappointing her son.

With all this emotional chaos in his life, it was no wonder that Jeremy acted out some of it at school. When he had a bad day, many adults at school had an equally hard time of it. He was especially surly when he was tired, hungry, or cold. Mondays were particularly difficult because he was allowed to stay up late to watch Sunday Night Football. And if the Pittsburgh Steelers played and lost, look out.

But one saving grace was that we could talk about the game. Of course, we didn't talk directly *to* him while he was in the middle of a tantrum. Instead, our assistant principal and I would talk *past* him, to each other, about things Jeremy would love to be consulted on—such as whether Big Ben Roethlisberger really should have risked going with a slant to a fumble-prone tight end on third and three. Jeremy would soon give up on the tantrum to join us in conversation. He couldn't help himself.

The key is that we were distracting him with a subject that genuinely interested him. This is a technique teachers use all the time—capture a child's attention with a "shiny object," then take advantage of his attention to focus him where you want him to be. It takes time and patience. That's why we use a team approach, so teachers can keep teaching while the support group—in this case, Team Jeremy—steps in to get the wheels back on track.

Trevor's Story

Here is an example of how knowing a student's backstory can not only help reveal why they do what they do but can also help leverage a solution to a thorny problem.

One morning, I was at a school district meeting when two high school principals excused themselves and rushed back to their respective campuses to quell escalating tension between black and white students. The provocation for these incidents came from white students who were using the Confederate flag to inspire animus. Reports of the flag being hung in public places on or near those campuses had prompted swift action by the principals and district administration. We elementary and middle school principals at the meeting were cautioned to be on the lookout for similar copycat behavior at our schools and to do whatever we could to stay ahead of it.

But I wasn't overly concerned about what would happen at our school. *I've got this*, I thought. Why? First, those two high schools in question were in Beaufort, way on the other side of the district from ours. Further, this latest ploy by white students to harass African Americans involved not only flying the Confederate battle flag but wearing it as well. Our information was that many white students throughout the district planned to wear shirts with Confederate flags on them that day. However, my confidence arose from the fact that although not all schools in those days were "uniform schools," ours was, meaning that our students were required to wear khaki pants and either a red, white, or yellow polo shirt. School communities voted to be or not to be uniform schools. Prior to our opening, the Bluffton Elementary community chose to join our sister school, Michael C. Riley Elementary, in being a uniform school. Individual families could opt out of the uniform policy by signing a waiver. But we strongly discouraged that—it defeats the purpose of the uniforms—and we were gratified when only three families opted out. On the day of the school district meeting, I thought the flag wearing, at least, wouldn't be an issue because the vast majority of our students wore uniforms. What could go wrong?

When I got back from the meeting, just after noon, I smiled when I saw a group of students waiting patiently in a line near the front office for their teacher. Typically, the students stop there on their way to or from related arts classes or lunch while their teacher checks her mailbox. She rejoins them moments later, and they resume their trip back to the classroom.

As they waited, I saw a third-grade student named Trevor Perkins wearing a yellow T-shirt. He was the only child not in uniform as his family had opted out of the policy. There was a message on the back of his shirt, something about Southern heritage. Even before he turned around, I knew what I would see on the front of that shirt—the image of a Confederate flag. This was a Dixie Outfitters T-shirt, made by a company dedicated to showing pride in Southern history.

Sigh. While some people say that the Confederate flag is a symbol of Southern heritage or the fight for states' rights, my view is that it is symbolic of slavery, segregation, and inequality—and sometimes animosity and hatred. Beyond that, we had just been reminded at our morning meeting that any display of Confederate symbols in our schools was prohibited. In any case, the flag, which had been adopted by racists and white nationalists as an emblem, was totally off-limits at Bluffton Elementary and all the rest of the schools in the district. Yet there stood Trevor wearing it.

I had known Trevor to be a sweet, decent child, quick with a smile. He got along with everyone. He was eager to help classmates and teachers and loved anything to do with life on the South Carolina shore, just as his parents and brother did. As I looked at him, I formulated a plan for talking to him about the shirt, believing that he had no idea why wearing it was a problem.

First, I took his teacher aside to ask why in the world she had allowed him to wear that T-shirt with an outlawed symbol on it. After all, it was well after noon; hadn't she seen it earlier? Her answer was, "Yes, I saw it, but I didn't know what to do about it." I didn't like that answer. Besides, we had an assistant principal who was not notified; she would certainly have handled the matter appropriately.

"Hey, Trevor. How are you?" I asked. "Are you having a good day?"

Trevor smiled at the attention he was getting from me. He always did. Then, for the next twenty minutes, Trevor and I had a conversation about the symbol on his shirt.

I asked if he knew that the symbol was hurtful to some people and therefore something we didn't allow to be displayed at school. He didn't seem to know anything about that and in fact seemed concerned about it. He didn't like the idea of wearing something that might hurt someone's feelings. Indeed, for all 180 days of school, while nearly everyone else wore a red, yellow, or blue polo-type shirt with khaki pants, Trevor usually wore a T-shirt of some type with camo, plaid, or solid-colored shorts. But he had never worn a Dixie Outfitters shirt in the past.

I could have easily demanded that he remove the shirt and wear one of many uniform shirts we had on hand as extras for other students. I could have told him who is most affected by such a symbol and why, a story I could have laid out with no trouble and in little time.

But instead, I asked him what *he* thought we should do about it. Did he plan to keep wearing the shirt the rest of the day? If he had said yes, I would have suggested another answer, but he said, abruptly, "No! I shouldn't do *that*. And I won't wear it to school anymore." As before, I didn't think he completely understood; he was deferring to me. I said it was a problem, so he believed it was a problem.

"What should we do next? We have uniform shirts for people to use. What do you think?"

He shook his head, indicating that wasn't a possibility. "My mom said to never wear a uniform shirt. I'm not supposed to ever trade my shirt for a uniform shirt." We can infer from this that (1) his mom was a racist, (2) she didn't think the act of wearing a Confederate flag was racist, or (3) she was interested in demonstrating her indignance over what appeared to be the school district's attempt to control what her children wear—or some combination of those things.

I said, "I don't have any other kinds of shirts. So would you consider turning yours inside out and wearing it that way for the rest of the day?"

He thought for a second, then told me that was a good idea and he would do it "right now." He then went to the boys' room so he could make the necessary adjustment.

I stood near the bathroom so I could speak with him when he came out. "Hey, Trevor," I said. "Do you think you're in trouble with me for any of this?"

He replied that he didn't know, but he was sorry he had made a mistake.

I told him that in my book, it doesn't count as a mistake if you had no idea there was anything wrong with what you were doing and that he most certainly was not in trouble with me.

That's the unique thing about young humans: they have an innocence and naivete about so much of what their parents make them do. And sometimes they are used by their parents.

The only thing left to do was talk to Mrs. Perkins.

After answering the phone and hearing my voice, she greeted me with more negative energy than I would have liked. "Are you calling to tell me you're suspending my son from school for his shirt?"

Ah. There was so much meat in that statement, with a side order of gravy to come.

She went on to tell me that her older son had been suspended earlier that day for wearing the same T-shirt. Clearly, she had seen to it that both her children would be dressed in a way that would bring negative attention to them—to the point, perhaps, of marketing them as racists to their classmates. I didn't know whether the older son was aware of this, but Trevor didn't know what it was all about and likely would not have wanted to be a participant in what amounted to a protest at best or an intimidation campaign at worst.

I answered that of course Trevor was not being suspended from school for wearing the shirt. I told her that Trevor and I had reached an agreement about the shirt, and all was well. We talked a bit about what would happen if the shirt showed up again—which it never did, nor did any other item of clothing that might have been considered provocative.

Then she said, "Well, those jerks at that other school suspended my older son today, and I'm gonna sue."

Sigh again. So she set up both her boys as canaries in the coal mine to see if we "jerks" would take the bait and suspend her boys. I didn't qualify that day as a jerk by her reckoning, but I did embark on a fool's errand when I tried to explain that the suspension of her high schooler might have a lot to do with the fact that the warring factions had gotten more chippy than usual and to warn her that someone might actually get hurt over such perceived slights. I am nearly certain I got nowhere on that score, but I did learn some years later that in a discussion of the way in which I dispatched my duties, Mrs. Perkins pronounced me "fair." And I'll take that any day of the week.

Ben's Story

Of course, as an involved principal, I try to help students with whatever they're going through, no matter how big or how small the issue might be.

For example, there was a second grader, Ben, who lost one of his baby teeth at lunchtime. He put the tooth on his tray but forgot about it, then after lunch he threw the contents of the tray into the garbage. When he realized what he had done, he was crying hysterically.

Armed with rubber gloves and aprons, I told Ben that he and I would dig through the trash together to look for that precious tooth. But we couldn't find it.

Although Ben was quite a strong child—often a bit of a pistol, even somewhat arrogant—this mishap revealed how vulnerable he was. Because he was so upset, I decided to write a letter to the tooth fairy on his behalf. And I made it look as official as possible, complete with a wax seal. I then instructed Ben to put the letter under his pillow that night, after he explained to his parents what happened at lunch.

I wrote:

Dear Tooth Fairy,
My name is Dr. Corley, and I am the principal of Bluffton Elementary School. Ben lost a tooth today. He was very eager to share it with you and put it under his pillow tonight, but he accidentally threw it away at lunch. We looked for it together,

but we couldn't find it. I am sending you this letter to verify that he did indeed lose a tooth.

Ben's parents no doubt read my note, and the next morning, he found six dollars under his pillow. Problem solved. And Ben's attitude going forward? He toned down the arrogance, displayed a bit more humility, and had a warm smile for nearly all of the adults with whom he came into contact. Coincidence? I think not. Rather, the leverage of a shared experience.

CHAPTER 3

Mentoring and Training

My Journey from Teacher to Principal

HOW DID I LEARN THE BASICS OF UNDERSTANDING AND communicating with children? You might say I was thrown into the pool at the deep end and forced to swim.

Having spent almost a decade as an elementary school music teacher, I became an assistant principal at age thirty-one under somewhat odd circumstances. During the 1980s, none of the elementary schools in our Palatine, IL, district had assistant principals until our superintendent decided to institute the position in its five largest schools.

A light bulb went off in my head. I had always done what I could to make the school where I taught run smoothly. So why shouldn't I strive to be an assistant principal? The transition from teacher to principal really appealed to me. I had frequently been able to help other teachers relate to their students. They could see that I made it a point to be available to children and was open to having conversations with them whenever they wanted to share something with an adult.

At that point in my career, I wanted to increase my sphere of influence beyond a single classroom. I believed I had an innate leadership ability and an instinctive understanding of our students. I wanted to offer those qualities to the school district in a broader way.

My Career in a Nutshell

Experience

September 1979–June 1987: Music teacher, Community Consolidated School District 15, Palatine, IL

July 1987–June 1991: Assistant principal, Thomas Jefferson Elementary School, Community Consolidated School District 15, Palatine, IL

June 1991–July 1994: Principal, Heritage Elementary School, Lynchburg, VA

August 1994–June 1999: Assistant professor, Graduate School of Education, Salem State College, Salem, MA (later, Salem State University)

August 1994–June 1999: First principal, the Saltonstall School, Salem, MA

August 1999–September 2007: First principal, Bluffton Elementary School, Beaufort County Schools, SC

September 2007–April 2009: Academic Improvement Officer, Beaufort County Schools, SC

April 2009–present: First principal, Red Cedar Elementary School, Beaufort County Schools, SC

Education

1978: Bachelor of science, music education, University of Illinois, Urbana-Champaign

1984: Master of music education and administration, Chicago Musical College of Roosevelt University, Chicago

1994: Doctorate, educational administration, University of Illinois, Urbana-Champaign

In addition to my teaching experience, I had also recently completed coursework for a master's degree in music education and administration. I would eventually get a doctorate in educational administration, but armed as I was with my teaching credentials and a master's, I immediately applied for one of the assistant principal positions. And much to my surprise, there was a figurative wrestling match between two principals who *both* wanted me to join them: my current principal, Mike, at Willow Bend Elementary, and a principal from the other side of the district, Al, at Thomas Jefferson Elementary. These two men could not have been more different.

Details are sparse about exactly how the decision was made, but it had something to do with Al convincing Mike that Al would do a better job training me than Mike would. I knew only a bit about Al. Chief among those things was that he was demanding. So I was apprehensive about this turn of events.

Mike was a passive sort of guy, more of a manager than a leader. He kept the trains running on time, so to speak, and administered the school with competence. He was friendly and personable with his staff and students. But a planner and organizer he was not. Paradoxically, I did more to prevent disciplinary issues than he did because he wasn't proactive enough in setting boundaries or communicating his expectations. Yes, he was approachable, but he did not have high standards for students' behavior.

Al, on the other hand, though soft-spoken—unless it served his purpose to be otherwise—was bold and decisive, a force to be reckoned with. Though he ran his student body of eight hundred with military precision, he did it with a thoughtful touch that garnered him undying admiration from school employees and respect from parents and his colleagues in the district.

Al became my mentor. And he took that job ever so seriously. As I would observe after I was hired, he was an operational wizard. No matter how complex the task, he could draw up a master plan for it, design a procedure, and communicate the details to teachers and staff, generally in a way that resulted in unanimous agreement that his plan was preferable to any other suggestions. He would ask for feedback and adjust accordingly. Yes, he knew curriculum, instruction, operations, and leadership. That was a given. But he was also intuitive about what mattered most.

One of Al's talents was seeing through the peripheral static that often impedes vital functions in a school. With a laserlike focus, he analyzed classroom protocols and student performance data at a time when others at his level barely acknowledged that such data existed.

In those days, test scores, time-on-task statistics, attendance information, and anecdotal records from teachers about student performance were available but not analyzed and not used to improve instruction. Al absorbed all this with ease. He also understood the pressures that teachers face and was kind to them if they made a mistake. The course correction was always made in private—no shame involved.

In short, he treated everyone with utmost respect, though he could still be managerial and firm. That was his magic. He was a master at it.

Staff drama happens in all schools, right? Not that one. Although all the teachers and staff members were female except for the social worker, there was never any of the condescension you would sometimes find when male administrators led predominantly female teams. There was something about Al's body language and facial expressions that said, "If it's not for the good of your students, it's got no place here."

When it came to his relationship with the students, Al was generous with his time. Most importantly, he truly listened to students and was listened to *by* them. The beauty of this was that mutual respect existed without fear. (Actually, there *was* a bit of fear—the fear of disappointing him. I believe we all felt that.)

The man had his playful side too. He never missed an opportunity to add some levity to the school day. Every once in a while, he would play a trick on the teachers and secretly entice the kindergartners, one by one, to leave their classroom and join him in the hallway. The idea was for Al to spirit as many children out of the room as he could before the teachers figured out they were missing. I believe his all-time record was six children. Their disappearance was facilitated by a long half wall where their little coats were hung. And more than once I saw Al crouching down to get at eye level with his "catch," all of them reveling in the game. But to be fair, I'm pretty sure that the two kindergarten teachers knew exactly what he was doing and let him believe that he had outsmarted them once again.

Although Al wasn't tall in stature, one always got the feeling that he was the man in charge. He gave me the sense that he likely spent the first half of his life trying to convince the people around him that he was taller than he really was by having such a presence. His athletic stance, take-charge posture, and commanding way of speaking helped him pull off this feat. Yet when he was crouching down with the littlest of our students, bringing himself to their eye level, in my opinion, he was never taller.

Maxims to Live By

My mentor, Al, led from a base of firm moral convictions. Among them were:

- Say what you mean and mean what you say.
- Be firm but not rigid.
- Students come first, above everyone and everything else.
- Teachers come in a close second as they endeavor to make their classrooms interesting, safe, and inviting.
- It is the principal's job, often with the help of other people, to remove anything that stands in the teachers' ways.
- When challenges arise, look for what is *not* there as well as what is.
- Make sure that everyone who crosses the school threshold feels safe and heard.

- If it feels wrong, it likely is.
- There is no better job in education than a school principalship because it is the last, best place to effect change at the person-to-person level and improve lives through quality education. My doctoral adviser at the University of Illinois frequently echoed these sentiments as well.
- Actions have consequences: though cause and effect often elude children, they need to understand that once you push something out into the universe, what comes back at you might not be exactly what you anticipated. And you cannot control that feedback either.
- Children can accomplish anything if you support them in their efforts.
- Take care of problems before they take care of you.

One of the things I admired most about Al was that it was obvious where he stood on most every issue. Teachers, parents, and students knew what he valued, and amazingly, the majority of them amiably complied with his wishes, if not always championing them.

During the three years I worked under Al's watchful eye, he was the perfect mentor for me. And I often count myself quite lucky that he won the "wrestling match" over me. To this day, whenever I'm faced with a dilemma, I often ask myself, *What would Al do?*

Brandon's Story

Parents sometimes turned to Al even years after their children had left our school. For example, one couple came to talk with him about their teenage son, Brandon, who was a sophomore in high school at the time and had once gone to our school. They were concerned because Brandon had recently taken up smoking. "Mr. Hopkins," the mother said, "Brandon seems to be making bad choices, and he won't really talk to us. Would you talk to him?"

As the parents confided in Al, I watched Brandon from the window of the main office. He was sullenly slumped in the family car. When he was asked to come in, he didn't look like he was headed to the gallows, but it was clear he didn't believe he was picking up free concert tickets either. He did a pretty good job of acting tough. I imagine his self-talk went something like, *Yeah, no big deal. So he was my principal when I was ten. What's he going to do to me?* He almost had me sold on that facade.

Over the course of the next twenty minutes, I wondered if Al, the fix-it man, would have the same impact on Brandon as he did on students who were much younger. After the meeting, as Brandon left Al's office, I observed the teen's demeanor. There was Al, standing in his office doorway with his hands on his hips, striking a hero pose while maintaining an air of intro-spection about him. Clearly, he had bonded with Brandon in some way when Brandon was his student and he had just leveraged that bond to triumph over the problem. Meanwhile, Brandon's face clearly gave away the mantra he must have been silently repeating: *I'm not going to cry.*

Time was frozen for a moment. Brandon moved past his parents and headed for the exit.

"Brandon," Al said. "Aren't you forgetting something?"

Brandon turned around, walked to the spot where Al stood with his hand outstretched, and placed an open pack of Marlboros on Al's palm. Then he quickly left the school. Slow clap. Boy, did I have a lot to learn.

Everything about Al's effectiveness that day had been years in the making. First, Mom and Dad trusted him. Second, Brandon likely feared but respected him. And interlaced with that fear was the knowledge that Al genuinely cared for him. I imagine he was thinking, *Mr. Hopkins was always there for me even when I messed up, so I'm going to listen to him now; I have to listen to him.*

In short, Al accomplished a character reboot with Brandon because of the relationship he had established with the boy years earlier.

Report Cards

Another thing I learned from Al was the immense value of keeping tabs on a student's grades and writing an encouraging remark on every child's report card. To this day, I continue the practice, as do most of my mentees. Even during a year when there were more than a thousand students at one of my schools, I wrote on *all* the cards. True, it's a lot of work, but the benefits outweigh the costs by a significant margin. These remarks send the message that the principal cares enough to write something personal to each student. Another benefit is that the teachers also notice this effort and put even more time into writing their own comments.

For a student who is doing well, I'll write a few sentences adorned with smiley faces and exclamation points, generally expressing my admiration for their achievements or progress. For students who aren't doing so well, my comments are substantially longer. I encourage those students to be the best they can be, laying down a specific challenge—something they can and should accomplish the next quarter and beyond. My goal is to remind them that they are capable of anything they put their minds to and that we, the members of their "tribe," are there to support them. Fifth graders get the longest and weightiest of my comments, because around midyear, I'm already thinking about how much I'm going to miss them when they move on to middle school, and I'd best make the most of the time we have left together.

Nearly all parents appreciate the effort. But on occasion I run afoul of parents who object to my comments. How dare I challenge their children? When that happens, I remind the parents that my comments are always made in a constructive spirit—a hopeful and we're-in-this-together mindset. I try to understand their objections, but I never relent. I will always keep writing. And I always direct my comments to the child, not the parent, *because the child is our client; the parent is not.**

A few times, parents have objected to a comment I've made on a report card conveying my belief that everyone has choices and that doing one's best work is one of those choices. The parents in those instances felt that their children really did not have choices and were unable to do their best. I agreed to disagree and moved on.

Corleyisms

* You have just encountered a Corleyism. What is that, you ask? It is an expression I am known for using that relays one of my core beliefs. I have been told by colleagues that they turn to these expressions whenever they find themselves in a difficult situation and are in a quandary about what to do. When I contemplated writing this book, I wondered, *Hasn't everything worth saying already been said?* Many told me, "No. Your Corleyisms alone could fill a book!" That was the ultimate compliment. I am aware that some of these expressions have been ingrained in our school culture, although I must confess that I am also known for the most god-awful puns as well.

Below are just a few of my favorite Corleyisms:

- "In a perfect world, we wouldn't have to reach out to this family on this issue yet again, but it isn't a perfect world, so we must."
- "When I mess up, I own up. Sometimes that's the way it goes: if you can't be anything else, be a bad example."
- "Some students will never know a thing exists out there in the world unless we are the ones who bring it to them."
- "Students don't care how much you know until they know how much you care."
- "Everything a child does happens for a reason. Find out the reason, then meet the need. Don't just deal with the behavior."
- "Some students come to school to learn. Some come to be loved, then they learn."

Finally, there's an expression that, while not a Corleyism, is one I and many other administrators have used for years. It goes, "Don't complain about the students some parents send to school. They don't keep the 'good kids' at home; they send you the best ones they have."

My variation on this goes, "Don't complain about these parents. The students bring us the best ones they have."

These report card comments, combined with our other established best practices, such as paying close attention to nonverbal clues, attending students' musical performances, analyzing data about them, talking with them, bringing together teams to assist them as necessary, and following up—both with teachers and counselors and with the students themselves—allow all of us to make inroads with children who need as much encouragement as they can get. Because my comments are supportive, children are receptive to talking with me. It is much easier for a child to talk with an administrator about something unpleasant if that child has some sense that the adult is and has always been in his or her corner.

In essence, the children and I leverage our relationships with one another to work through whatever needs attention. With trust and mutual respect, we can face whatever challenges arise. I have not cornered the market on this approach. Everyone who has been at Red Cedar for at least a few years feels this way: we all know one another, we care about one another, we share the same values, and we are confident that we can accomplish great things together. Some might say we are mission-driven. Those people would be correct.

Staying in Touch

My contact with students does not end when they graduate and go on to middle school. They leave behind indelible impressions. And my sense of caring for them does not stop either. After elementary school, I sometimes see former students at school football games or working at local restaurants. Years later, some of them even end up student-teaching or ultimately becoming a full-time teacher at our school. One way I continue to track former students may seem a bit odd. But I assure you, I do it only for the most positive reasons.

There is a website operated by the Beaufort County Detention Center that displays daily arrest records and posts the mug shots of people (other than minors) accused of various crimes. I make it a point to regularly scan this site, and if I find a former student on it, I write that person a letter.

But first, I find the student in the appropriate yearbook so I can look at his or her photo. Why? Because looking at a child in the days of his or her innocence is the best way to capture the charm, promise, and adorableness I remember. I then make a copy of the picture and attach it to the letter, in which I describe the most positive things I can recall about that child. And then off it goes in the mail.

Although the response rate is not high, when former students do respond, they usually stop by the school in person. And they typically express their appreciation for their experience at our school and make a promise not to repeat their "really stupid behavior." That was the phrase used by one of my favorite former students, a boy named Thomas, who had been arrested for disorderly conduct and driving without a license.

Thomas's Story

I remembered Thomas as a bright student with a ready smile who loved to care for animals, a passion he shared with his mother. One day at school, during recess, I remember seeing him on his way to the school nurse's office. He was holding in his hands a butterfly with a broken wing. The seven-year-old wanted to know if the nurse could give the butterfly a "cast or something." Though some bully in his class was making fun of him for being so sensitive about the butterfly's well-being, Thomas didn't care and was ready to fight the bully if necessary.

The day I saw his photo on the mug shot site, I wrote him a letter reminding him of what happened that day and lauding him for being so kind. I also expressed my hope that his arrest was a one-off and that he would be more responsible in the future, refocusing his attention on what was important in life—for instance, putting casts on butterfly wings—rather than getting arrested.

Not long after I wrote the note, I ran into Thomas's mother at the supermarket, and she greeted me warmly, happy for the chance encounter.

I had no intention of raising the topic of her son's arrest or my letter to him. But she knew all about it. "He's here with me, and you two should talk," she said. And just at that moment, Thomas came around the corner and saw us together. My first impression? He was so tall! I hadn't seen him since he was in the sixth grade, but now he was entering his senior year in high school.

"Hey, Dr. Corley. How are you?" were his first words to me.

His mother glanced at him. "We had a conversation about what you wanted to tell Dr. Corley if we were to see her, right?"

Thomas nodded, looked at his shoes, and said, "That was really stupid behavior, and I am never going to do anything like it again. Thank you for the letter you wrote me."

Then he looked at his mother as if to say, *See? I did it.* I told him that I was convinced he meant what he said and would support him in any way I could. Thomas kept his word, and at last report, he is doing well in college, on his way to becoming a veterinarian.

Who would have thought that my letter would have mattered to Thomas or his mother? But it did. When this kind of connection is made, it reinforces the concept that there will always be a staff member at school who will care about students. This feeling of security is a true game changer. Do I believe that my letter made him change his behavior? No, not really. That's because I believe he was already headed back on the right road. But maybe my letter helped him validate that making a change was the right thing to do.

When training new or aspiring teachers, I therefore try to impress on them how profoundly educators can affect a student, making a difference in ways they cannot predict. Young educators need to hear this the most. The more experience they have, the more likely they are to have this epiphany all on their own—well, with the help of the students, of course.

But there are certain parents who are impervious to any educator influence. In fact, there have been times when I was certain that even after *years* of trying to get a point across to a parent, we got nowhere. One of those times really stands out in my mind.

Carter's Story

Ashlie Barnes, a teacher fresh out of college, looked quite upset at the end of her first Meet the Teacher Day.

"I think I did something wrong," she told me, looking quite depressed. "I said something to a mom about the behavior of her son Carter, but I don't think I did it right."

Carter, one of Ashlie's new kindergartners, had walked into the classroom with his mother, mischievously grabbed some papers that had been neatly stacked, and threw them in the air. He then pushed a chair to the floor, looked at his mother, and just laughed.

His mother's response? The wrong one. She laughed, too, then said, "That's my son—the class clown!" Her letting him off the hook that way, excusing his bad behavior, was not going to fly in our school.

My unspoken response to hearing this was my signature *Sigh*. That is, I don't actually sigh; I say the word *sigh*, as though I'm reading the script of a play. "And then what happened?" I asked Ashlie.

Slowly and quietly, she said, "That's when I kind of fake-laughed and said, 'Yeah—but not in *this* class.'" That was pretty gutsy for a first-year teacher, and I liked her instinctive reaction to set a boundary.

For sure, what she said needed to be said. This boy was not amusing and was accustomed to being indulged by his mother, who clearly had no idea how to control him. In our school, his disruptive behavior would not be tolerated, not even in kindergarten.

Of course, the mother was probably embarrassed and defensive about her inept handling of her hyperactive son. We knew we had a challenge ahead of us—to get Mom to work with us and do what was best for Carter. Both mother and son needed to understand and abide by our expectations for behavior in the classroom. It wasn't easy getting this point across.

That first year was difficult. Carter did not like sharing toys or attention with other children and had trouble following directions. If he didn't want to sit still and listen to Ashlie read a story, he would just run around the room and distract everybody. If he didn't want to do math, which he never did, then he completely ignored it. Not acceptable.

I must say that Ashlie worked hard in her outreach to Carter's mom. This young single parent needed to care more about Carter's behavior and help him follow the rules. She had to understand that by doing this, she could help us build Carter's self-confidence and belief in his abilities. The staff at the school, Team Carter, supported Ashlie's efforts in any way we could. Although we used every opportunity to encourage, cajole, and reward Carter's mother whenever she cooperated with us—celebrating even the smallest improvement on her part—we pretty much failed because she didn't take our efforts seriously. The road was long and slow.

Things didn't get much better for Carter in the first, second, third, fourth, or fifth grades. Sure, he was a little better at complying with his teachers' requests, and he half-heartedly completed his assignments, but we never succeeded in creating a desire in him to be his best. Neither did we foster in him a spirit of inquisitiveness or some semblance of wanting to make anyone, including himself, proud.

As time passed, disappointingly, Mom never got on board with "the whole school thing" (her words during one of our uncomfortable conversations). Instead, she believed that we were just picking on Carter, making him the victim. Even when the parents of some of his classmates attempted to reason with her, she blocked their feedback. She also dodged our phone calls.

For Carter's part, he understood that we cared about him, and there were even some instances when he was quite empathetic toward his classmates, though he resisted the idea of school in general.

A few years after Carter left our school, I was attending a meeting at the district office, which also houses our alternative school. This school is for students who have forfeited their opportunity to continue at their zoned middle or high school because of poor behavior choices. But there was Carter—a taller version of his elementary school self. He greeted me appropriately, if not warmly.

"Why in the world are you *here?*" I asked.

He explained that he had gotten into a dispute with another student in the hallway at the middle school, and there were some other things he had done that earned him suspensions, so he had been assigned to the alternative school for ninety days.

As always, he played the victim: "That assistant principal had it in for me. He always makes a big deal out of whatever I do." Not true, I was to find out later. It was the same old impulsive Carter, lacking self-control and a sense of appropriateness, choosing unwisely, and blaming someone else for his problems.

Some years later, Carter's little brother, Anthony, was registered at our school as a prekindergartner. I was not looking forward to history repeating itself and feared that might be our fate. However, after a parent-teacher conference, this is the report I got from the teacher: "Mom told me she wanted to make something very clear. She said she had 'dealt' with you before and knew that you don't put up with nonsense when it comes to how kids act in school or how parents react to critical feedback."

A knot started to develop in my stomach. I believed that Mom and I might indeed be settling in for round two—that nothing had changed with regard to our differences about the way a child should behave in school.

"She assured me that things were going to be different this time around. She said she was young when Carter started school and she thought she knew everything. She didn't like you acting like her mother, telling her what to do. So she wouldn't listen to anything you said.

"But she's changed. She said she was not going to make the same mistake twice and was going to ensure that Anthony behaved and did his work. In fact, she indicated that she felt lucky to get a second chance with you."

Well, that was unexpected! People really can change. That did wonders for my incipient stomachache.

True to her word, Anthony's mom attended to Anthony's education in a thoughtful manner. And believe it or not, Carter was a big part of that. He had changed schools a few times, eventually graduating from an alternative high school a few states away from his home, and ultimately became a good citizen and student. He was now a great example to his little brother, seemingly born into the role. This gave me hope. Something we had done with him in elementary school had finally registered, and his behavior had transformed.

That phrase about taking a village to raise a child? It applies to parents too. Perhaps it *does* take a village to raise some of them.

We All Just Want to Have Fun

Metaphorically and literally, most four-year-olds tend to want to pick up rocks to see what's under them. They are likely to be naturally curious about their surroundings and search for understanding about what they experience.

Unfortunately, educators often work at cross-purposes with this innate inquisitiveness, which might, if left to itself, drive a lesson to its logical conclusion. We are bound to our own agenda: "Yes, Andrew, that is a great rock you have there, but we're working on phonics right now, so you need to put that down. Maybe we'll talk about rocks a little later."

But we rarely do.

To capture Andrew's interest, we could launch the whole class into the geological equivalent of an Easter egg hunt and toss out a perfectly good lesson plan in favor of what some people might view as a flight of fancy. And in that same classroom, what about Clara's budding love of Arabian stallions? Should we, can we, how would we pursue learning about horses along with anything else that stimulates learning in that class? No. It's not practical.

Somehow, educators need to strike a balance between both these priorities—cultivating children's natural curiosity and mastering important learning objectives. Good teachers maintain high levels of engagement in their students while at the same time teaching what their students need to be learning. When we can capture students' attention in the moment, we can gain important academic ground and use that momentum to steer the child to a memorable learning moment. In the long run, we can develop enthusiasm around learning. Children anticipate the lessons ahead: "I can't wait to see what's next!"

Enter fun, stage left.

It started with an idea inspired by the Perfectly Princess Tea Party at Disney World, where children can fulfill their fantasies—for a price—by attending a tea party with a Disney princess or two. I'm very much not the princess type, but I thought, *Shouldn't every child have the opportunity to live a dream—whether it be captaining a ship, piloting a plane, leading a team of scientists, or solving a mystery?* The answer, of course, is yes. And this kind of experience shouldn't be reserved only for those who can pay Disney's ticket price for such a thing.

You may be thinking, *Well, back in the day, my friends and I made forts with sheets and blankets and pretended we were cowboys.* Today, though, for any number of reasons, not many students do those kinds of things. But I believed that if we gave our students at Red Cedar the opportunity to choose one of four "worlds" they wanted to join for an evening, and if we fully immersed them in that experience, we would create something magical, even life-changing (at least until we could top it somewhere down the road). At the same time, we could engage some of our staff in creating a special event all of us would remember for a very long time. We named it Just My Imagination.

I chose four staff members whom I thought would be interested and inspired. I had a plan firmly in mind for the event and what each of the worlds might look like, but I didn't share those details with anyone—not even the four staff members I'd invited to create those worlds.

I asked each member of the team to consider what kind of world he or she wanted to create and what and whom they would need to help them accomplish it. My proposal was met with stunned silence, then nervous laughter. It was a lot to take in. But the team members got over that quickly. Each of the four "creators" agreed to join this crazy plot and planned for weeks to make the big night special. They enrolled their grade level tribes in the effort and placed their food and staging orders with me.

The evening of the soiree, a staff member in costume met each of the students as they were dropped off at the school by their parents. The "concierge" checked her roster for each student's name. Did we know that some of them would never see Disney World or anything like it? You bet we did. That's why we made every effort to make invitees feel special—as if they were on the VIP list! The students were delighted: creativity abounded and opportunities opened for them to exercise their imaginations.

- Benji Morgan, our music teacher at the time, announced at our first meeting that his creation would be all about comic book heroes and villains engaged in a struggle between good and evil. He was pretty sure he could get a few friends to help, including one who was studying drama production at the Savannah College of Art and Design and who would be happy to sew costumes for the students, repurposing cast-off clothing. *Costumes?* What a great idea, one that I would never have dreamed we could consider.
- Lori Willis, an upper-grade teacher with a huge heart for the students who need it most, is a lover of all things pirate. It was no

surprise that she decided to create the bow of a pirate ship in our media center with the assistance of some of her grade-level teammates, other staff members, and her husband.

- Michelle Morrison, one of our literacy interventionists and the leader of our special services team, made outer space her imaginary playground. Her team of "astronauts" managed to narrowly escape all kinds of celestial dangers throughout the evening, employing every space-inspired sci-fi motif in the book as they did it.

- Cynthia Laizer, then our academic coach, created a castle motif and affected a British accent for the event. Her environment required some fast talking on the set-design front. We convinced the maintenance folks that we needed some scaffolding in the cafeteria, then we covered it with butcher paper and tried to make it look like the turret where Rapunzel let down her hair.

Did we all have fun? Yes, we did. The creativity in food and staging surprised even the adults. The imagination and the acting skills were amazing. The costumes elevated everything. It was a great evening. An exceptional amount of effort was put forth by the relatively small group of people who made it happen.

The adults talked about it for weeks afterward. The children brought it up far longer than that. For all of us, the experience led to greater connection and engagement, which in turn led to positive outcomes in the classroom.

One of the boys, a very quiet third grader who originally signed up to be a hero in Benji's world, expressed some unease when he arrived on event night. I struggled to find a place for him that he would enjoy. So I told him I could really use his help serving the food to all the groups.

"It's complicated, Steven. I need some help keeping it all straight. Could you give me a hand?"

He thought for a moment and said he was pretty sure he'd be really good at that since his dad was a restaurant manager. He was right. He was attentive to the "patrons" in each venue. He played his part as if he were born for the role, even affecting a lower timbre in his voice and a bit of a dialect, though I'm still not sure which one.

At the close of the evening, the adults were dead tired. One by one, the students rejoined their parents in the parking lot, mostly talking nonstop about the events of the previous few hours. Some of them were also happy to explain why they were dressed in what used to be men's workout shorts and were now, clearly, swashbucklers' britches.

Steven was the last child to be picked up. On his way out the door, the boy looked back at us and told us he had really enjoyed the experience. He took a few more steps and said thank you. Then he added one last comment: "We can do this again next week, right?" That there, my friends—that right there—is everything.

Every day, for every child, to the extent that it's possible, there should be something at school that makes life awesome and inspires a love for learning. Magic is optional but preferable.

Speech 137

It's a familiar scene: A crowd of parents slowly shuffles into the school auditorium. Standing offstage, I hear scattered coughs, seats shifting, the low murmur of people talking, and maybe the rustling of programs. As always, I make sure the staff involved give me the high sign before I walk to the center of the stage, tap the microphone, and begin what I call Speech 137.

No, there are not 136 other speeches preceding this one. I picked the number at random. However, the official-sounding number does make it memorable. It's a speech I present every time parents attend a school event, whether they come to watch their children sing, dance, play an instrument, perform in a play, or receive an award. I give the speech at performances of the Foxes Jam ensembles, a collection of stringed and wind instrumental groups we instituted with the support of the Hilton

Head Symphony Orchestra.[5] I also give it at performances of the Foxes Rock Drum and Dance Team. (We are the Red Cedar Foxes, with Foxy as our mascot. Nearly all our many clubs have the word *foxes* in the title.)

It's a positive speech, and it contains no admonishments. I don't say, "You know you really ought to" a single time, though I've been known to at least imply that on other occasions.

As I announce that I'm about to begin Speech 137, I notice some of the parents warming up to it. If they've attended other student events or performances, they've certainly heard it before. I watch them smile and get comfortable. If they sit next to someone who hasn't heard the speech in the past, they direct that person to listen with a nudge and a glance toward me. They know the newcomer will like my trademark speech.

Let me tell you a secret: there's nothing truly remarkable about the speech—except that it's on a twenty-five-year streak. I give it every time there's an audience in our auditorium. The speech varies in length, depending on how well it is being received, how long it has been since the audience has heard it previously, and how eager the students and their teachers are to get the show started.

Here is the basic version:

> We are so happy that you could be with us here tonight. Your children have been practicing for this night for a long time. You've probably heard them rehearse some of the music they will perform. I know that there are a lot of places you could be tonight. You all have busy lives with many demands. But you chose to be here to watch your children perform.
>
> Some children feel very proud to show you what they've been working on. Others feel a bit reluctant to perform. But either way, your presence makes a difference to them, as it does

5   For more information, see "Youth Programs," Hilton Head Symphony Orchestra, https://www. hhso.org/youth-programs.

to us. It tells them that you value what they do in every facet of their lives. That's really great.

Please continue to do what you're doing right now when your children get to middle school and high school. That's when your children need you the most and act like it the least. They might well encourage you to put a bag over your head if you tell them you're coming to their performances. Do whatever you need to do—but go.

My colleagues in middle school and high school would give anything to have an auditorium filled with parents and grandparents. You might or might not know that children stop playing the violin when they sense that their parents really don't care about it anymore. Maybe the parents did at one time, but not now, so why should the child? Plus, your presence here extends your ability to influence your children. After all, they have friends, YouTube, TikTok, and fifty other things vying for their attention every single day. All that means there's less space for what *you* want them to know, the choices *you* want them to make. To take advantage of one more opportunity to be there is in your best interest.

Watch, listen, and engage with what they do. Please, continue to support your children in all they do. If you do it consistently, there will be a day when you're talking with your grown-up child on the phone, and she says to you, "Hey, Mom, I have to go now. The kids have a program at school tonight, and we want to get good seats." Then you will know you have taught them well.

Thanks again for being here for them. Please enjoy the show.

The unabridged version of this speech also includes a shout-out to older siblings who come along to attend the performance. I compliment them on their loyalty and remind them that someone likely did the same for them when they played a very squeaky clarinet or danced in a manner they wanted everyone to forget—now that they're the coolest age they'll ever be. The warmth from the families is palpable.

We all know that people are busy and life is hard. Some of our parents work three to five jobs between them. If they have made it to school, it's a big deal and should be celebrated. These are the good times. The speech reminds parents of this and honors them accordingly.

Often, parents of students who graduated long ago will call or email to let me know about the first time they heard me give Speech 137. They tell me they enjoyed hearing it and that it stuck with them. Later, when they thought about skipping an event, they ended up going. Or when their children told them they might not want to participate in an event, they invoked my name, and that did the trick. Regardless of whether it was a superlative performance, they shared an experience as a family— which usually leads to another experience and another and another.

As for me, I love to see our students doing what they enjoy and feeling proud of performing in front of their parents. Many times during a program, I have split my attention between appreciating what the students are doing and watching their parents absorb it all with pride. And I've told them so. When committed and talented adults who care about their children set high expectations for artistic and academic performance, the results often blow them away. The secret ingredient is the parents' consistent participation. That's the heart and soul of Speech 137.

PART TWO

Breaking the Mold: Launching an Innovative New School

CHAPTER 4

The Salts I

A Shared Leadership Approach to Elementary School Education

THE SALTONSTALL.

It has quite a regal ring, doesn't it? From the sound of it, you might be tempted to think it's a luxury hotel in Somethingshire, England.

But this elegant-sounding name actually refers to a remarkable elementary school in Salem, Massachusetts. Sometimes just known as the Salts, it was the first school where I functioned as the founding principal. And it turned out to be a career-changing experience that paved the way for many of the innovations most dear to my heart.

I became aware of the job opening at the Salts through an ad in *Education Week* in late 1993. At the time, I was principal of Heritage Elementary School in Lynchburg, Virginia. I gleaned from the ad that the civic leaders in Salem were committed to the concept of a new school predicated on philosophies that were important to *teachers*. Had I still been a teacher, I would have wanted to be part of something similar. The prospect of being the leader of such a school was even more thrilling. So I applied for the position of principal at the Saltonstall, though the teachers and community members were uncertain that they would call the chosen leader by that title as it might be too traditional a choice for this forward-thinking school.

I also did some research. I learned that the Saltonstall was named for Leverett Saltonstall I (1783–1845). He was a member of the US House of Representatives, a member of the Board of Overseers at Harvard, president of the Massachusetts state senate, and the first mayor of Salem, Massachusetts. The school that bore his name was just as majestic as the man himself.

The building, having stood proudly on Lafayette Street since 1916, had once been a beautiful Federal-style brick structure—three stories tall, located just a few blocks from Salem Harbor. By the time I saw it, it clearly was not at its best, though there were big plans underway for a makeover.

Originally constructed on the ashes of the Great Salem Fire of 1914, it had been a K–8 school for most of its life. Later it became a middle school known as Middle School East. By 1993, much of it had deteriorated; its beauty was diminished by the ravages of time and weather. The wooden floor of the gym had buckled from water damage. The two-story arched windows in the once grand auditorium had been covered over with plywood. The decorative plaster molding that adorned the ceiling was missing some of its dentils, and its paint had peeled.

Then, in 1994, a miracle happened. Funding from the city of Salem, supporting an expansive renovation that would restore the structure to its original luster and add a bit more space, became available. In addition, the state provided funds in the form of time and learning grants, supporting the vision of a very determined and imaginative group of teachers.[6]

---

[6] Time and learning grants encourage groups to find ways to make the most of and/or extend learning time in creative ways. For a similar program, see "Grants and Other Financial Assistance Programs," Massachusetts Department of Elementary and Secondary Education, https://www.doe.mass.edu/grants/2022/225.

Educational Innovation

Further, in 1993, the United States Department of Education, under a program called Fund for the Improvement and Reform of Schools and Teaching, began offering grants to pay for major initiatives in public schools throughout the country. The funding was substantial, but so were the stringent qualifications for potential recipients. One of the many requirements was that the funded initiative be the product of a partnership between a school district and an institute of higher learning. For any school to have a chance at receiving a grant, it needed a great leader to forge such a connection.

Enter the two heroes of what was being called "the new school at the Saltonstall": First, there was Ed Curtin, then the visionary superintendent of Salem Public Schools. In his desire to do the best he could for the children of his hometown, Ed always led with his heart.

And then there was Dr. Nancy Harrington, who was the equally bold Salem State College president. Together, their goal was to encourage the coupling of a dynamic school district with a progressive college or university for the purpose of instituting a revolutionary educational program in an elementary school setting.

Salem overperformed in that regard by planning a school that would put into practice research-based educational initiatives devised by the teachers themselves. Their participation was a very big deal, and Ed Curtin insisted on it.

Indeed, trusting the teachers to engineer an optimal school protocol was considered an enormous leap of faith on the part of Curtin, the school committee (which most states refer to as a school board or a board of education), and the city of Salem leadership. Truly, to this point, it was unheard of to have a committee comprised mostly of teachers compile a ten-page list of everything they were absolutely committed to having in their school. The teachers at what was then called the new school at the Saltonstall did that and more. They led the conversation and did the research to support their choices. Those teachers were not just on board for this one. They were at the controls. This was new. This was different. This was important and exciting from its very beginnings.

As circumstances dictated, the building would need to be vacant for a year to allow for the completion of the $6 million renovation.[7] This meant that whoever was hired as the new principal would have a full year to plan the rollout of the school without any responsibilities for administering an academic year in progress. In other words, without a staff or students to manage, this new person would have the luxury of time because the school wouldn't open until the following year.

That's where I came in.

I was thrilled to have secured an interview, which took place on the evening of the last day of the search. I actually planned it that way. I thought it was preferable from an impression-making point of view to have the "final" word.

Cutting it kind of close, I took the last flight of the day from Lynchburg to Boston. At the airport, I rented a car and drove straight to Salem High School, the self-styled Home of the Witches. (It said so on every sign and school-spirit item I encountered along the way.)

For the interview, I wore a red silk suit with brushed gold buttons— small buttons, not too gaudy. It was kind of a "Well, here I am; I've got nothing to lose and everything to gain" sort of move. Always being the punctual sort, I arrived in Salem with forty-five minutes to spare. (My doctoral thesis adviser always told me to celebrate the small victories. This, as I saw it, was one of them.) I was ready for whatever they had to throw at me.

---

7 The school operated as Middle School East until the renovations were approved. Then the Middle School East students were moved to what had been the old Salem High School, then housing Middle School West. Later, Middle School East merged with Middle School West to form Collins Middle School on that old Salem High School site.

The interviews took place in a conference room that had floor-to-ceiling glass walls separating it from an open waiting area. As I arrived in the waiting area, I noticed that the privacy curtains in the conference room were drawn. They were thick enough to obscure the features of the people behind them—just their silhouettes were visible—but not thick enough to block all the sound from that room. Suddenly I was no longer feeling so self-confident.

Once I took in the atmosphere, I felt a bit intimidated. I could hear people in the conference room laughing at what seemed to be some kind of private joke, and the person who was clearly the interviewee was laughing the loudest. This person was distinctly comfortable in this setting. Swell. Things were going too well in that room. I worried that I might not be able to establish the same rapport.

I asked myself, *Am I following a hometown favorite? The candidate they really want?* Maybe the interviewers were just going through the motions of a national (and intergalactic) search for the optics of it all. I returned to the red silk suit mantra: "Nothing to lose; everything to gain. Here I am; let's see what happens."

But in the end, my interview went quite well. The team was impressed with my understanding of what they were trying to accomplish. They liked my deference to skilled teachers and my agreement with the notion that what goes on in a classroom is the most important discourse there exists on the planet. I also was on board with the idea that a large part of this school's success would have something to do with CPUs and keyboards.

In short, I liked them; they liked me. After they completed their due diligence, I was offered the job. It was time to move to Salem, Massachusetts. So in the spring of 1994, I fulfilled my contract in Virginia and was ready for a new adventure.

Time Warp

Right after my interview at the Saltonstall, I experienced a culture-shock moment as I strode down the cobblestone walkway of the Essex Street pedestrian mall. Just as I reached for the receiver of a pay phone that was conveniently located in a kiosk on the mall, I was approached by two young women wearing Pilgrimish attire.

"Going to the Witch Trials today?" one of them asked me.

Oh, my. I'm in Salem. *That* Salem. I was so focused on being in the right place at the right time and making sure I did the best job I could in the interview, I gave no thought at all to the significance of the city I was in. "Um, no," I said. "Not today. I have to tell someone that I'm going to be a principal here in a brand new—I mean, not *brand* new, but a school that isn't open yet."

What a ridiculous response that was, even though it was completely accurate, especially as it was offered to actors who were portraying nosy Salem townsfolk circa 1692.

"Maybe tomorrow, then," the actress said. "They'll be on all week, methinks."

I was amused by this, swept up in the moment. *Clearly I'm not in Lynchburg anymore, methinks.* So this little town, so rich and rooted in seventeenth-century history, was about to jump headlong into a new and groundbreaking adventure in education. Amazing dichotomy when you think about it.

Switching Gears

I liked being a principal at Heritage Elementary in Lynchburg until I learned how to do it. Then I loved it. I mean I *really* loved the job—as in born-for-this loved it. And although I was successful in the role, I was far from remarkable. In Salem, I'd have so much to learn.

Every district operates differently. Every state operates differently. I would need to become familiar with the staff, the needs of the students, the demands of the parents, the values of the superintendent, and the culture of the district as a whole—all daunting prospects taken together or separately. In Lynchburg, I had made mistakes and tried to learn from them. Sometimes I missed the mark. And now? Now these good people were going to trust *me* to help fine-tune their mission and vision. Whoa. Breathe...

Somehow, I was the person who was going to implement the state-of-the-art, best-practices-based school-management protocols established by the Committee for the New School at the Saltonstall while overseeing the renovation of a dilapidated three-story building. Moreover, I was going to be the one to pitch parents in the community on the school's merits. Because Salem was and is a "choice" school district, families in the city can select the school they want for their children. Some parents of students who were already attending other schools were skeptical because what we were offering was quite a departure from what they were used to. Many of them were wondering if all the innovations were as promising as their proponents said they would be. (More on those innovations in a bit.) But it was my responsibility to recruit the families whose children would attend the school—which had a capacity of approximately four hundred students—all while learning the ways of a new-to-me district.

Oh, and for good measure, I would also become an assistant professor at Salem State College, an institution for which the Salts was to become a laboratory school, joining the Horace Mann Laboratory School, located on the college campus.[8]

Again, I thought, *They really think I can make all this happen. Did I oversell myself?* Just weeks before I was a less-than-seasoned administrator. Yet they had picked me. *What did I say in the interview that made them choose me? Never mind that now. You're in it. You can make this happen,* I reasoned to myself.

I do believe that people can rise to any occasion for a cause they feel passionate about. To give myself a boost, I remembered my trusted

[8] In 2010, Salem State College became Salem State University.

mentor, Al. He would likely have had some sports analogy to offer, something like "You miss 100 percent of the shots you don't take."

Well, one lesson I learned from him is that an educator can surmount any challenge if she has focus and determination. And as the new set of challenges was spinning through my mind, I thought, *What would Al do?* Fortunately, I was able to place a few phone calls to him and benefit from his wisdom.

In addition, to accompany me on this new adventure, I had the unwavering support of my soon-to-be husband, Wayne, whom I had met at a lecture at Lynchburg College (now the University of Lynchburg). He was a real estate developer and community leader in the city and my lifeline during this challenging period.

Before my arrival at the school, many decisions had already been made—those concerning the renovation of the structure, the delivery-of-instruction choices, age groupings, class sizes, and school colors. But most everything else—all the operations and logistics decisions—was up for grabs; they were puzzles waiting to be solved.

Perhaps surprisingly, that was music to my ears. I have always wanted the largest playpen possible when planning for instruction. (Most teachers want the same.) To this day, I am known to request clarification before convening a strategy group: "Do we have any rules that govern this matter?" If the answer is yes, I ask, "Whom should I talk to about *massaging* those rules?" If the answer is no, I'm on to the trailblazing phase, just as soon as I can complete the pleasantries.

The first item on my agenda was to meet my suitemates in the basement of Collins Middle School—the Parent Information Center (PIC) staff. As I mentioned, Salem had adopted a school choice plan, a voluntary program designed to desegregate the city's elementary schools. No matter where a family lived in Salem, parents could opt, or "choice" (used here as a verb), into a school that was not in their neighborhood if they felt its programs were a better fit for their children. The PIC helped parents make those choices and was responsible for administering the process. It was a logical place for me to set up shop and meet with prospective parents as well as a legion of others during the construction year at the Salts. That's where I met the captivating and driven Perla Peguero, who worked at the PIC as a district-based outreach coordinator. When we created a role for her at the Salts, she became our parent liaison.

As I soon discovered, whether speaking in English, French, or Spanish, Perla had a way of warmly communicating that put families instantly at ease. She was a master at breaking down barriers between parents and school personnel. This was especially true for immigrant families, for whom differences in language and culture can obstruct communication with principals and teachers.

Perla was a formidable thought partner and a great help to me in all the meetings in which she participated, and I learned a lot from her. For example, when she had a long list of information to present, she delivered it in digestible bites, with lots of space in between for questions. She also wisely met with parents informally, in a café atmosphere, which established instant rapport. In short, she was our secret weapon when it came to informing parents about the many benefits we could offer their children. And it soon became clear that we were basically interviewing each other for the opening of the Saltonstall to see if we truly wanted to spend our days together for the foreseeable future. Spoiler alert: we did.

Next up on the agenda was a series of meetings with the Committee for the New School at the Saltonstall, which had been working on this project for more than a year. I was really inspired by the quality of teacher-generated initiatives from this impressive group of motivated and experienced educators. As I well understood, good teachers know what is best for their students.

And this new school was going to reflect that truth. But as I also understood, even when teachers get the blessing of their bosses, there are always twists and turns along the way, prickly problems that may seem insurmountable. Yet teachers show superhuman strength and perseverance: they blow up those construction cones, make it work, and submit an annotated report shortly thereafter that details how they pulled it off.

What came out of those meetings before and after I arrived was an articulation of the school's mission in a document titled "Philosophies and Programs Present in the New School at the Saltonstall"—a ten-page, single-spaced position paper that was our version of Martin Luther's Ninety-Five Theses. It included our "must-haves":

- students would be grouped in multi-age clusters;[9]
- the teaching techniques would be those of our own design;
- students would be taught a second language as part of their regular course of study;
- instruction would follow Howard Gardner's theory of multiple intelligences;[10]
- every kindergartner and first grader would take violin lessons rooted in the Suzuki method;
- there would be a year-round, or "balanced," school calendar;[11]

---

9   That is, kindergarten and first-grade students were grouped together, and the teacher remained to welcome new kindergartners the following year to join her new first graders. Second and third graders learned together, and fourth and fifth graders did the same. Staying with the same teacher for two years has great benefits. Being the younger and then the older in a class has advantages as well—not to mention the benefits of having fewer transitions.

10   This theory posits eight types of intelligence: visual-spatial, verbal-linguistic, interpersonal, intrapersonal, logistical-mathematical, musical, bodily-kinesthetic, and naturalistic. See Kendra Cherry, "Gardner's Theory of Multiple Intelligences," *Verywell Mind*, updated October 19, 2022, https://www.verywellmind.com/gardners-theory-of-multiple-intelligences-2795161.

11   This means that students would attend school year-round, without the traditional two months off during the summer. Some schools opt for a "45-15" schedule, meaning that students attend school for forty-five days, then have the next fifteen days off. For more information, see Grace Chen, "Year-Round or Traditional Schedule?," *Public School Review*, updated November 30, 2022, https://www.publicschoolreview.com/blog/year-round-or-traditional-schedule.

- students would learn self-efficacy initiatives;[12]
- students would have access to several computer labs in the building;
- decision-making would be shared among teachers, administrators, and staff;
- there would be a Friday Club that would hold special-interest classes for students; and
- teachers would have dedicated planning time every Friday.

To my mind, every one of our principles had to be articulated as precisely as possible. We needed to clarify the promises we were making to families and other stakeholders. And ultimately, we needed to define our brand—that is, we needed to explain what we stood for and what distinguished our school from all the other schools in the district in order to help parents select the best school for their children.

But What Shall We Call You?

At one of our many planning meetings at the Saltonstall in the fall of 1994, Betty Rea, a longtime teacher at the Horace Mann Laboratory School, remarked, "You know, at first, we wanted to be self-governed, so we didn't want a principal or 'head' of school as such. But now that we do have you, most of us think that since we are a 'break-the-mold' school, the leader's title should be completely different too."

I was somewhat taken aback by Betty's comment, which I assumed was a dig meant to cut me down to size. So it took me a minute to reel that in and analyze what it meant. I tried not to think about the implication that the teachers were grudgingly tolerating my presence.

---

[12] The American Psychological Association's definition of self-efficacy is "an individual's belief in his or her capacity to execute behaviors necessary to produce specific performance attainments." See "Teaching Tip Sheet: Self-Efficacy," American Psychological Association, https://www.apa.org/pi/aids/resources/education/self-efficacy.

While I was digesting all this, another committee member, who likely took in my dazed and confused expression, added, "What Betty means is that we didn't really want a 'principal,' but they said we had to have one, so..." This was not getting any better.

Committee member number three, Marilyn, a teacher at Witchcraft Heights Elementary School (yes, that's its name, and it's located on Gallows Hill), took a stab at it. "We know we need a principal, and we are happy to have one—I mean, happy to have *you*. The thing is that we don't like the title *principal*, so can we talk about that?"

I agreed that we could talk about it for sure, though my title really wasn't a priority because there were so many other things to do in terms of planning. I thought, *The weight of the Western world does not rest on this issue. It does not need to be resolved in this moment.* So I tabled it.

But the topic resurfaced some months later. This time I was prepared. When the matter came up, I said, "I've got it. I know what I would like my title to be: *archangel*." (Stage direction: *Ten-second pause*.)

For good measure, I struck a guardian angel-like pose, arms outstretched, head slightly tilted upward. The room went silent. The committee did not know how to react. Had they just hired some sort of loon? Was this error reversible?

I didn't let the consternation go on for more than a minute before admitting that I wasn't serious, though the title *archangel* would look spectacular in an email signature.

"Here's the deal, friends," I said. "Whatever title we use must pass the Joe Lunchbox test. If, for example, you decide on *headmistress*, I believe parents would boil that down to what it really means. They might say, 'Headmistress. That's like a principal, right?' My answer would have to be yes. 'Then why don't you just call it that?' they might reasonably ask. And I would have no satisfactory response."

There was silence again—my kind of silence. I think the committee learned a lot about me in those meetings, as I learned a lot about them. And we never talked about the title thing again except to joke about it. I think what they most worried about was that some of the teachers would lose their authority by giving me the title of principal. But somebody has to be the leader in every school, and I was it. If a few people resented it, they would just have to deal with it. Besides, someone, such as a principal, has to contend with buses, behavior, quartermaster activities, and all the other things that teachers are not delighted to do. We call those things "administrivia."

The Construction Phase

While all that was happening, I met regularly with the clerk of the works for the city of Salem, Bob Gauthier, who was often at the school overseeing the building renovation. He was good at his job—uncompromising, thorough, and self-assured—though he could also be a bit intimidating. So could I, which is perhaps why we got along so well. Please be assured, though, that he was significantly more intimidating than I without trying at all.

I understood a little about construction thanks to my dad, who was an ironworker for the American Bridge Company and, following that, a self-employed crane operator. He could understand how most anything was designed and built. Also, in previous years, I had supervised three school construction projects, including a new wing for one school and a complete rebuild for another, so all that experience helped me gain some of Bob's trust. Whatever challenges arose, we found ways to resolve them together.

Fortunately, I never crossed the forbidden line of asking for a so-called change order, an expensive reversal of construction design. Never, ever do that. There were few crimes worse than this in Bob's mind—and in those of every construction manager I have ever known. That commandment has served me well throughout my career as a principal. And the little things you pick up along the way often frame the questions asked and decisions made on the next project.

For example, one wise decision when it comes to construction in school bathrooms is to use poured concrete floors rather than ceramic tiles. That's a must, because if there is any kind of grout used, urine will eventually permeate it, and custodians will have a devil of a time getting the place to smell minty fresh. Aren't you glad you know that now? Ah, the glamorous perks of building schools.

What's more, as I learned, if you must have a drop ceiling in restrooms, make sure the drop level is beyond the reach of your tallest student when he's standing on anything made of porcelain—such as a toilet or a sink. Otherwise, you will have created a convenient hiding place for contraband such as cell phones and skin magazines. The learning curve is steep on the facilities side of things. The struggle is real.

Union Negotiations

Because of key changes to our calendar year at the Saltonstall, three union contracts had to be renegotiated. These negotiations would affect teachers, classified staff,[13] and custodians. All this was necessary because one of our tenets at the Salts was that a year-round, or balanced, calendar was essential to optimal learning, and the existing union contracts contained no provision for that kind of schedule. As if that weren't enough, we also wanted to add an hour to the school day, ten days to the student calendar, and twenty days to the staff calendar, all of which required contractual amendments.

Unfortunately, our negotiations with the unions came on the heels of a teachers strike, so the mood was not entirely in our favor from the

---

[13] According to the United States Code, classified staff is "an employee of a nonprofit entity who works in any grade from prekindergarten through high school in any of the following occupational specialties: (a) paraprofessional, including paraeducator services; (b) clerical and administrative services; (c) transportation services; (d) food and nutrition services; (e) custodial and maintenance services; (f) security services; (g) health and student services; (h) technical services; (i) skilled trades." This is distinguished from certified staff, who require certification or licensure to perform their jobs.

start. Making it more challenging was the fact that I didn't have any background in labor negotiations. It's lucky I didn't need it.

My job, as I saw it, was to keep my mouth closed during bargaining meetings and speak only when I was spoken to. That I could do. The attorney for the school committee rephrased any questions directed at me unless they were extremely straightforward. If one of them felt like a trap, he might even raise an eyebrow at the questioner. Once the attorney recast the question, I answered it.

Getting to where we needed to be took months and required a surprising amount of emotional energy. There were times when things seemed promising. There were also nights when our time together dragged on and on and we accomplished nothing except to increase the tension in the room. One night, the union representative for the clerical staff was visibly upset by something that seemed to me quite innocuous. He put all his office supplies back into his briefcase, harrumphed, and made his way toward the door. Then he stopped, only to sit by himself in the chair closest to the exit.

We all took that in, not knowing what to make of it. Our attorney looked at the teachers union leader and said, "Hey. Your guy can get up and storm out of the room, but nobody gets up and storms *almost* out of the room. It just doesn't work." He then suggested that we call it a night and reconvene in two days.

I felt quite a bit of pressure as I observed the union representatives present at the meetings. They took detailed notes about what we said and no doubt pored over them after the meetings to see where they could gain some advantage. There is also the possibility that all that note-taking was done for the sole purpose of unnerving the school-committee side of the table.

One person took notes whenever the school committee's attorney spoke, and another took notes whenever the superintendent answered a question. The woman who was writing down my comments even noted when I drank some water or put my pen down. *Really? No, that can't be.*

Let's test that theory, I thought. I crossed, then uncrossed, my legs. Yep. Back to the notebook. *Oh, no. This could be dangerous.* Consider, if you will, the amount of self-restraint I exercised resisting the temptation to perform some sort of jujitsu move or yoga pose to confirm that the woman would feverishly write about it.

This was particularly tempting once the negotiations devolved into a contentious phase. Sometimes there were cooling-off periods, and some meetings were called to an early close because we had reached an impasse. All along the way, the stakes were quite high: our new school was not going to open unless these deliberations were successful.

But by around the seventh meeting, things started to even out, and the light of hope was visible on the horizon. Soon thereafter, everyone reached the necessary agreements. Compensation, of course, was the major bone of contention. An extra hour per day, twenty extra days per year: that's a lot more time on the job for our teachers—well over 20 percent more than what was provided for in the contract that all the other teachers in the district had signed. Eventually, we agreed to a 17 percent increase in salary. The rest of the differences were mediated. This was an enormous milestone.

By the time the grueling negotiations ended, I had learned quite a lot—not the least of which was a pearl of wisdom from Anne LeBlanc, who would serve as our media specialist and a kindergarten and first-grade teacher at the Salts. The teachers union contract at the time was printed for its members in the form of a small, thick, squarish book with a red cover. I was reading it one afternoon and was struck by the specificity of it, sometimes to the point of absurdity, or so it seemed.

I asked Anne why there was so much minutiae packed in that little thing. She took the book from my hand, glanced at a few of the pages in the middle, reacted negatively to one of them, and with a slight "Ya gotta be kiddin' me" expression, looked at me and said, "I can see why you might think some of this doesn't belong here. But what you don't know is that every time we asked for raises and didn't get them, they gave us *something*—anything they could think of—instead."

So every single thing in that book had a reason behind it and therefore a monetary value. Perspective is important. Thanks, Anne.

Roland Barth, Education Expert

When I was educating myself about running the Salts, I was inspired by Roland Barth, the founder and first director of the Principals' Center at the Harvard Graduate School of Education and the author of *Improving Schools from Within: Teachers, Parents, and Principals Can Make the Difference.* It was sort of a bible for those of us in the school administration realm at the time.

I wrote him one day on a lark, explaining that I had been named principal of a new and innovative school, not very far away from his old teaching and learning grounds. I wanted his help so that I wouldn't miss any of the important steps along the way as we planned a school from the ground up.

Dr. Barth was retired by then, but he graciously answered me in November of 1994. He dated the note "Late fall sometime." What a marvelous way to put that. I decided that I, too, would someday date my correspondence in such a manner.

Along with many other nuggets of wisdom, he pointed out that the cohesiveness of our project would likely be most vulnerable just before the staff was chosen. As he explained, that's because regardless of how fabulously promising the outcome might be, there were always going to be staff members who harbored a very different vision of success. People who had been our staunchest proponents might begin to withdraw, feeling less enthused about the project, even betrayed.

Dr. Barth further explained that while people are preparing for a project, little differences might be there, but they are not obvious. Once the staff comes on board, however, two things happen: One is that those little differences get played out into actions, and the result is not what everyone thought it would be. The second is that once the people who are going to operationalize the vision start to do it, there might be snags that make some of that great plan unworkable. So the height of satisfaction for some is just before the christening, not just after.

This advice offered a cautionary tale. Fortunately, although there were schools in the Saltonstall area, especially charter schools, that thought they had satisfied the planning group members but had not, and where deep divisions occurred that doomed some of those efforts or put them at severe risk, there were only a few people in Salem who appeared to feel as Dr. Barth predicted they might.

CHAPTER 5

The Salts II

Measures of Success

THE EXCITEMENT AND ANTICIPATION SURROUNDING THE opening of the Saltonstall School was building in the community. By the late winter of 1994, the union contract was settled and the path cleared for a fall opening. Thereafter, I divided my time among construction supervision, speaking with anyone in the community who would listen to our vision, and interviewing teachers to fill the available spots.

I can tell you this: there was no shortage of teachers who wanted to work at the Salts, so there were a lot of interviews to conduct. On that last score, I was permitted to observe teachers as they plied their craft in their current classrooms. This was very revealing, allowing me to see these teachers in action and assess what they did best. In nearly all cases, I was blown away. The teachers who sought to join us at the Salts poured their hearts into their lessons. And don't think I was snowed by any dog and pony show. I knew by that time, based on students' reactions, what was a regular occurrence in a classroom and what was not.

These teachers, the ones who eventually joined us at the Saltonstall, were the real deal.

We had completely staffed the school by early spring. And it was then that we ran into a major snag. To my dismay, I learned that the renovation to the Saltonstall would not be completed in time for a fall opening. Well, that changed some things—did it ever. It became a bigger "construction cone" than we would have liked, but the school district, working with the city of Salem, came up with some alternatives.

Interestingly, I did some research and found a 1916 article about the building's opening back then, which was delayed because desks and chairs were held up in a train station near Saint Louis. If only the problem were so simple this go-round.

As for our situation, the solution was to house the fourth and fifth grades at the Horace Mann Laboratory School and establish a temporary school for the rest of the students at St. Anne's, a Catholic school in town—which at the time was being used for weekly Thursday night bingo games. To create a classroom environment, we erected makeshift partitions to prevent distractions and to somewhat muffle the sound. The partitions were packed up every Thursday afternoon in anticipation of bingo night and at other times to accommodate the occasional spaghetti dinner.

However, placing and replacing folding chairs every Thursday afternoon and Friday morning caused some agita for die-hard bingo purists. "Lucky chairs" were not to be disturbed: the rule ostensibly dated back to the days when bingo arrived in Salem, perhaps as early as colonial times. We were chastised for breaking long-standing bingo winning streaks with our cavalier chair placement. We apologized and promised to do better.

The agreement with the archdiocese included a clause specifying that there was to be no recess outside on a day when there was a funeral. Obviously, hearing sixty or so children loudly enjoying their recess time was not going to be appreciated by grieving families and friends entering and leaving the church. And requesting that the little people "keep it down" during their soccer game was just a bit unrealistic. So we adjusted and remained flexible, adapting to our odd set of circumstances.

There was also a "fall bazaar" clause in the rental contract, meaning that we had to find alternative classroom space during Thanksgiving week, when the bazaar was taking place. We faced this challenge with creativity. We made arrangements to visit Collins Middle School and pair our classes with those already in place there. Melding our elementary school students with the older students was something some of us had always wanted to try anyway. It turned out to be a mitzvah.

Breaking the Barriers of Age

A few of our second graders who were attending a small special-needs class at the middle school identified with one of the tough-looking teenagers in that class who was trying just a bit too hard to market himself as cool. He dressed the part—dark clothing, leather boots, and perfectly coiffed hair, with lots of curls piled on top and sides that were nearly bald, in the style of a punk rocker.

I watched him because he seemed to be fascinated by a second-grade boy, especially when the little one tried out some dance moves to the beat of music that only he heard. The older boy, with a disarming smile, said, "That one's my guy," or words to that effect, indicating that he considered the boy his mate for the day. I understood what he saw in the boy: he had the same haircut and appeared to be the tough guy's Mini-Me. They both had a bouncy, athletic sort of stance, as though they might be asked at any moment to join a pickup basketball game.

During my rounds that day, the teacher of that special-needs class pulled me aside to tell me that the tough guy, Mickey, had shown her a side of himself she had never seen before. She said that having the younger students around provided an opportunity for him to let down his guard. She overheard him counseling his new young friend. "Ya don't wanna get behind in reading. They don't like that, and it's just no good.

Learn to read." The result was the best day he and she had had together and constituted what she believed was an inflection point on his path to making positive changes in his attitude and work ethic. She could use this as leverage with him.

In another example (this one occurred after we had been in our new building for around a year), one of our teachers at the Salts and a teacher at an alternative high school, which was for students who had not been successful in or had dropped out of a traditional high school, thought our second graders and the high school students could have some limited engagement with one another, as long as the second graders' parents agreed. We arranged it so that at no time would students be without both adult supervisors and two additional professionals nearby. In the teachers' view, the experience would provide the high schoolers the opportunity, much as it had for Mickey, to be childlike. For the second graders, it would be good to have high school students, clearly the coolest customers in town, read to them and pay attention to them.

During the lunch period, it warmed my heart to see the older students follow ours as they went together through the lunch line. They listened, and stifled giggles, as our seven-year-olds expressed preferences and "rather-nots" for some of the food on offer. I played the piano in the cafeteria, taking requests while I stole some glances in the direction of the three tables where the high school students were mixed with ours.

One young lady in the high school group had been flipping a closed milk carton slightly above the tabletop, as was the trend with water bottles among middle schoolers a few years back, much to the annoyance of the adults who witnessed it. She appeared to be trying to make it land flat side down. But when students started singing along to my piano accompaniment, her flipping of the carton ceased. She seemed surprised and pleased with the atmosphere in the cafeteria.

At the end of the lunch period, I played the "let's get quiet" song—the *Pink Panther* piece I'd always played to close out music classes years before.

As the cafeteria supervisor dismissed the first group of the students to their teachers, I walked over to talk to the high school students. I had a brief conversation with the young lady.

"You seem to be enjoying your day here. Yes?"

"Yeah. I mean, who wouldn't? This is kinda cool."

"What's cool about it?"

"This room is nice. It's pretty, and there's sunlight and stuff. And the kids are happy."

"Why do you think they're happy?"

"I don't know. Like, well, you're not yelling at them to do stuff, for one thing. Instead, you're playing the piano. Nobody played the piano at lunch at *my* elementary school."

I responded, "I want this to be a place where everyone feels safe and happy. I don't want to be yelling at anybody. Besides, they're not doing anything wrong."

"Maybe they're not doing anything wrong because you're playing the piano. They even wanted to sing the school song." She shook her head, taking in that thought. "I'm thinking, *Wow. Maybe if I sang at lunchtime and was happy at school—all the schools I was in—I wouldn't be where I am today.*"

School staffs must be incredibly intentional about what students experience under their care. Just about anything can be accomplished if it's the product of shared values and is carefully planned and prioritized. Student experiences should always remain in the consciousness of everyone who shares space in the school building.

In our case, our shared values were negotiated by interested stakeholders and widely publicized before we even had a building to inhabit. And we were all about the mission.

A Beautiful Building

Right before Christmas 1995, we finally moved into our beautiful new school—but just for one afternoon. I had to beg Bob Gauthier to finagle a certificate of occupancy for that single day. But we just *had* to be there for a very special occasion.

For weeks, Kris, our tireless, amazing music teacher, had been working on a production of *The Nutcracker*, which we thought would be a perfect way to inaugurate our new school. I will never forget the sight of a police escort leading a convoy of school buses through the snow from the Horace Mann Laboratory School to St. Anne's and then to Lafayette Street and the new home of the Salts. Teachers of art, music, and PE, along with office staff, were waiting at the front door to greet students, who carried all their school supplies in matching plastic tubs into the building and placed them in their brand-new classrooms.

It was the last day before the winter break, so it made sense for the students to bring their school belongings with them and put them in their classrooms before the performance of the play. Then we would be off for winter break. When we returned in January, we'd be in the new building on Lafayette Street for good.

Having waited so many months for the renovation to be finished, I must say that the final result was a triumph! The finishes on the building were stunning: all the detail work in the auditorium, around the windows and recessed into the ceiling, was done in period-appropriate lighter-than-pastel colors, no doubt rivaling the original 1916 splendor. Classrooms were a beautiful mixture of old and new. It was fascinating to see the bones of an early twentieth-century structure, complete with old-fashioned windows and ornamental flourishes, filled with modern classroom furnishings and the latest technology. Strategically placed floor tiles in the school colors—red, yellow, and blue—identified each grade level's areas.

The cafeteria, though located in the basement, was light and airy. This was because the school was built into a hill. The front of the building was on higher ground than the back of the building where the cafeteria was located. For this reason, even though you couldn't see the cafeteria from the front of the building, students could still walk out the back and be directly on the playground. The media center had vaulted windows that bowed outward to reveal the playground, the street behind the school, the field where the Salem State University baseball team played, and Palmer Cove, just south of Salem Harbor. In the hallway leading to the media center, we had three huge aquaria (one for freshwater fish, one for saltwater fish, and one for fish that prefer brackish water, which has less salinity than seawater and more than fresh water) along with a mural depicting brilliantly colored aquatic life—so the real fish would feel at home. It was a labor of love on the part of the art teacher and the science teacher.

Despite a few small speed bumps along the way, the school was a huge success. My dream of a child having something to look forward to every day became a reality for many.

School Spirit

It was very important to me that students feel a sense of pride in their school—a collective spirit of togetherness and optimism. And I believe that if you have any kind of talent, you need to share it, especially when you're trying to get a project off the ground. (If I may be immodest for a moment, my "go-to" skills involve music, humor, logistics, and the ability to inspire people. At the Salts, I used all this as much as I could.) So almost every day, on the piano in the cafeteria, I played a song that I wrote called "Saltonstall Pride," to which everyone sang along. High schoolers would come back to the Salts—still do, I'm told—and sing the song as they moved through the hallways.

"Saltonstall Pride" Lyrics

What's that feeling that you just can't hide?
I'd say it must be Saltonstall pride.

Doing our best, every day.

> Saying I'll try instead of no way.
> Making a choice, as you can see,
> To show caring, teamwork, effort, and responsibility.
>
> What's that feeling that you just can't hide?
> I'd say it must be Saltonstall pride.
>
> What makes us smile?
> What makes us proud?
> What makes us stand out in a crowd?
> The answer is here.
> It's you and it's me,
> Because we try to be the best we can be.
>
> What's that feeling that you just can't hide?
> I'd say it must be Saltonstall pride.
> Saltonstall pride, Saltonstall pride!

My repertoire included Disney songs, show tunes, and old rock and roll from the sixties. I took requests as best I could. And even though I'm a barely passable pianist, the students never seemed to care about that. They just loved the idea of their principal—any adult, I think—entertaining them, which is why I've played musical instruments in all my schools, whether for the students' daily arrivals and departures, before assemblies, or while waiting for a late bus to arrive. Not every day, of course, and certainly not as often as I would like.

In addition, as I do at Red Cedar and in every school I've led, I established and headed a drum-and-flag team, similar to the Foxes Rock Drum and Dance Team (always ably assisted by kindhearted teachers, bless them). We started at the Saltonstall in our second year, 1996–97, when we marched through the Willows section of Salem in the Horribles

Parade on the Fourth of July and through Salem proper in the Haunted Happenings Grand Parade in October. It was a great source of pride for fourth and fifth graders to perform "like a real marching band" with full-size drums, cymbals, bells, and flags. "Here comes the Saltonstall!" parents and other fans would cry from the sidelines, giving me chills every time I heard them.

When you're a new school, or you want to reinvent your school, you must institute activities, traditions, and events that bring people together and become a source of pride. These become your brand, the face you present to the world. At the Saltonstall, in the minds of community members—especially teachers who wanted to work with us and parents who wanted their children to attend the school—these traditions defined what we stood for and underlaid our school culture. You knew who we were when that drum-and-flag team came down the street. If you understood that, you could "speak Salts." It's like laying down a marker. This is who we are; this is what we do. And this is what you can expect from us and all who follow.

Bottom line: the values I hold dearest can be distilled in one word—*pride*. In fact, children playing on Salem Common could be overheard telling a sibling or playmate, "I don't think you're showing your pride" when that other child was misbehaving. On pride's coattails ride the Salts's core values of caring, teamwork, effort, and responsibility. Those four words encapsulate the school's culture, which remains alive and well today.

I can tell you that the initial enthusiasm associated with opening the school never really wore off. On the contrary, it grew stronger, especially among teachers and staff. We were in a palace of a school building, which was partly responsible for making the Salts *the* place to be. In fact, few teachers left to teach elsewhere. Similarly, few students left for other schools, and when they did, children on the waiting list took their places the following day.

Another expression of school spirit came about by accident. Remember our wonderful stew tradition at Red Cedar? Well, before there was Red Cedar Stew, there was Saltonstall Stew, and it was born out of necessity. In years past, the school calendar called for the Wednesday before Thanksgiving to be a full day of school. But when the school committee decided to dismiss the students midway through the day instead, it was good news. Families would have more time to travel to their relatives' homes for the holiday.

Ah, but there was a catch. There would be no lunch served for the students in the district that day. We decided that this situation was untenable. Enter Saltonstall Stew. Begun early in the morning and cooked in giant pots outside the cafeteria by staff and volunteers in what is usually freezing-cold weather, it provided sustenance for students at a time when the entire country was celebrating a spirit of plenty and abundance. And like any good tradition, it was improved on exponentially after I left. These days Stew Day is a full-on festival with games, loads of volunteers, crafting, and more. Is that good planning? Pride in the school? Magic? Yes, yes, and yes.

Standing Out

By the time our third year rolled around, we were at capacity, with full enrollment and another two hundred students on a waiting list. The media attention was a definite plus. There were positive news stories about the Salts in the *Boston Globe* and the *Salem News* and feature stories in school-facilities magazines and teachers union publications. A sitting congressman, Representative John Tierney, spoke glowingly about the Saltonstall on the House floor, and US senator John Kerry included accolades about us in a speech he gave at Northeastern University. Boston television news outlets and the *TODAY* show folks came to visit. School officials from all over New England requested appointments so that they could observe our teachers and talk with them about their craft.

It should also be noted that by the time a child reaches the fourth or fifth grade in a pre-K–5 school, the child and the family are pretty much settled in. They prefer to stay at the school the child already attends until he or she moves on naturally to middle school. So at the beginning, we assumed we might have one class of fourth- and fifth-grade students made up of the neighborhood children who would likely attend, but no more. The plan, initially, was to add a section or two of those upper-grade classes as the larger groups of students in the younger grades moved up.

However, we opened with an almost balanced school: we had nearly as many upper-grade classes as lower-grade classes. This meant that some parents of students in those upper grades must have had signif-icant motivation to change their children's schools. As we discovered, some children had not been successful in those other schools (or in more than one other school). Some parents were just looking for some-thing new and different. No one failed those students in the past, in most cases. The teachers and administrators just might not have found the right way to connect, or the family wasn't ready to partner with them.

So what was so special about the Saltonstall?

Was it the additional time we had built into the calendar and the daily schedule? Was it that we were the first public school in New England to have a year-round, or balanced, calendar? Was it our science and technology focus? Was it our embrace of Gardner's theory of multiple intelligences? Was it the strength of the certified and classified staffs? Our grouping of students of different ages in a single classroom, and keeping them with the same teacher for two years? Or the diversity of the student body?

All these components are part of what I view as best practices for teaching elementary school students. And it gave me a great sense of fulfillment to see those qualities recognized by so many children and adults looking for something different.

On the subject of diversity: the neighborhood immediately to the east of the school was known as the Point. Once home to French-Canadian cotton-mill workers, it later became a destination for a large contingent of immigrants from the Dominican Republic, who called the neighborhood El Punto. The Saltonstall became the local school for those Spanish-speaking children. Other students came from all over

Salem, including white, African American, and a few Asian American children. But the Dominican children came as a group. They knew one another because they lived on the same streets and in the same apartment buildings. They seemed to find some strength in that. They were brave. They were among the first students to walk the brick steps leading up to the heavy bluish purple doors of the Salts.

As I observed, the Dominican children, though unsure of their English skills, were not intimidated by their English-speaking peers. Indeed, they seemed happy and ready to learn. And no matter what their ethnic background, all the students at the Salts were emotionally open to meeting new friends and participating in the activities of a school that offered such an innovative approach to learning. Everyone, including the teachers, seemed ready for a new beginning.

Speaking of those teachers, they were incomparable in their creativity and industry, even surpassing the brilliant teachers I'd known at Heritage Elementary School in Lynchburg—where we simply didn't have enough of them to serve the complex needs of our student population. (At that point in my career, I wasn't prepared to "coach up" the teachers who needed it. I still needed some coaching myself.)

Teachers at the Saltonstall, on the other hand, had the advantage of generous financial backing, earmarked solely to feed our dreams at the onset of our existence, and total control of their classrooms. This taught me that when fine teachers are given the largest canvas available and 100 percent emotional support, they *want* to do amazing things for and with children. As is often said in education circles, these teachers knew their "why." It was also not lost on me that the same was true for the students. Our support for our Spanish-speaking students was overt, calculated, and widespread throughout the school. The teachers made it so.

They had a firm grasp of their craft from an academic standpoint, and more important, they cared about their students. I've learned that these sorts of teacher heroes figure out how they can relate academic content to each student, differentiating their teaching methods accordingly. And their students' academic growth, safety, and happiness are their why.

Our teachers were also unconditionally encouraging. Everything about their manner said, "You can do it!" They had mastered the art of truly listening and observing nonverbal cues. Some used wit and charm to engage students; others used an inviting smile that would hold students' attention.

I could cite countless examples of the Salts teachers and their superpowers. And they all learned from one another—and from me—just as I learned from them. The school was like a greenhouse for ideas, cooperation, and shared leadership. Somehow the mixture of temperature, humidity, nutrition, sunlight, and love was just right, allowing the magic to happen.

Passion in Action

I'll never forget when our second- and third-grade teachers at the Salts set out to teach their students about the Amazon rainforest. The teachers' skills were on display in full sensory glory. Because this was long before the availability of computers at every teacher's desktop, or YouTube videos for that matter, and since we couldn't take a field trip to the Amazon (yes, the teachers asked), they instead created a tableau at the school. It was spectacular, and clearly in these modern times, alas, would be against the fire code. Let's just say that it was an immersive experience, complete with the sounds of animals and other environmental ambience one might find there.

The reveal was exquisite. I watched the students marvel at what they were seeing and feeling: "Look over here! It's a parrot! Oh, wait! What's this vine? It's so thick! Ooh! Did you see that? Get the handout. We can identify it!" The children were mesmerized and could not stop talking about it. Moments like these are worth their weight in gold. They create indelible memories for students and prove that children learn when a teacher makes an emotional impact. This is what we did at the Salts.

No matter what the subject, teachers set out to create something extraordinary for their students. To say the least, they were not phoning in the curriculum, merely giving a robotic, textbook-dominated presentation. Instead, thoughtful preparation and imagination were the twin pillars of their approach, making the lessons come alive.

The teachers wanted to be given wide latitude to make their lessons authentic, compelling, meaningful, and memorable. They wanted to follow their imaginations so they could kindle those of their students. Another great example of this was the Winter Festival.

I tried not to look surprised when our soft-spoken music teacher, Kris, came to ask me about an idea she and her colleagues had—a science-arts-movement event. "It would be presented at night, with a full light show and lots of ice and ice-ish activities," she told me.

"Ice?" I stammered. "On the property, like for ice skating and such?"

Yes, that's what she had in mind. Ice sculptures, the building of which would be overseen by our art teacher, Jane Pace, would not be sculptures per se, because the words *carving* and *third graders* do not belong in the same sentence. Instead, ingeniously, the plan was to freeze several—and I mean copious quantities of—large cups of water, some with added food coloring and some without. The cup-shaped ice globs would then be fused together with a bit of water, then refrozen—God willing—in the front yard of the school. The structures would form at least one igloo and the border for the ice rink.

"Sure, Kris. Why not?"

To this day, I'm amazed that she wanted to do it and doubly impressed that she amassed the material, corralled the human assets, and devised the methods to accomplish it. And she was shocked and pleased that I said yes. What kind of joy-killing fool would I have been to say no to her? She became the driving force behind the project, which included acting as a human Zamboni, continually clearing the thin layers of snow that intermittently dusted the carefully tended ice. Before she left my office, most of the plan was in place, and my "note to self" was that I had better get busy and help find enough ice skates in various sizes to facilitate this adventure. (If you knew Kris Wilson, you would not be surprised to learn that she had already secured most of the skates before she made the request for the project.)

In yet another example of passion in action, one of our teachers, Kathy, kept trying to draw out a fourth-grade boy who was socially awkward and distant. Despite being a star math student, he solved all the problems in his head and didn't want to put anything down on paper. Kathy's goal was to get him to understand that if she couldn't see his work, she couldn't follow his logic. But before she could get him to do anything, he needed to trust her. Because he was shy and reticent, however, he seemed uninterested in connecting with either her or his classmates. This was a tall order, and Kathy tried every which way to make the boy feel comfortable enough to interact with her so she could help build his self-esteem.

One day, Kathy sent him to me right after math class. She wondered if I could talk to him in a way that might change his mind about showing his math work. I sat beside him as he wrote numbers in his spiral notebook. The page was crowded with them. I asked what he was doing. "I'm figuring out the distance from the earth to the sun in inches." Yep. That was Ryan.

I expressed my interest in the project and told him that I found it incredibly thought-provoking, but we had other work to do together. We then talked about his love of math, meandering our way toward the central question: "You know, Mrs. Adams would really like it if you showed your work when you do your math. Do you think you can do that?"

"No," Ryan told me. "I don't see why I should do that."

"But Ryan, your teacher has to be able to see your work in order to correct it."

Ryan stopped me cold. "But I almost never make a mistake, and if I do, I can just explain it." Well, then. He was right, after all.

But I had one more card to play. I leaned close to him, acting like what I was going to tell him was a secret. I looked around twice, then asked, "But what if Mrs. Adams should later be helping a student who is like you and tries the same strategies as you, but he's not as good. What then? If you could teach her how you think, then she could help the other boy. What do you say?"

I wondered if I got a base hit or struck out. Ryan put down his pencil and opened his eyes wide. "I didn't think about that. She should have told me. I could help her out, I think."

That was at least a triple in my book. It would have been a home run, but subsequent to our chat, he still wasn't consistent about showing his work. However, it was a great start.

As time passed, Ryan slowly emerged from his cocoon, becoming more verbal in class, helping his classmates, and participating in sports. Just two years later, he wasn't the same boy who entered the Salts. And he wasn't the only child transformed by the Salts experience.

Speaking of remarkable teachers and staff, let me return to our parent outreach specialist, Perla. From the moment she took up her position, she was a peacemaker, someone who advocated for fairness in all relationships. She was truly a master at holding a mirror up to people and allowing them to act in accordance with their better angels.

Perla was highly skilled at engaging traditionally underrepresented populations in school activities, acting as our emissary to the Hispanic community and so much more. Whatever the parents, usually moms, wanted to discuss with Perla was fair game. Most of the time they talked about the personalities of their children and their dreams for them, and sometimes about their own dreams too. From time to time, the parents also cooked and baked for us. But Perla was to perform one of her most memorable roles in an adventure involving an elusive spy.

Louie the Spy

One of the priorities in our founding document—"Philosophies and Programs Present in the New School at the Saltonstall"—was a program called the Friday Club, a weekly Friday morning event during which a large number of volunteers would share their special talents and hobbies with interested students. It was a win-win. Students learned everything from soccer and knitting to cartooning and city planning.

Meanwhile, the teachers would enjoy a well-deserved break from teaching, allowing them time to meet with other staff members and take advantage of that uninterrupted time for common planning, which was a huge gift, boosting their productivity and their morale. These meetings also provided important bonding time, especially because, by design, I was not in attendance, which meant that the teachers could speak freely.

In any case, I was usually leading a Friday Club session of my own, often on topics such as music and crafts. But my all-time favorite series of sessions was called How to Catch a Spy. Typically, around fifteen fourth and fifth graders would sign up. The idea was to catch a newly retired spy named Louie: he wanted to give back to the community by safely sharing the secrets of his craft. The students would try to locate Louie in one of eight major cities all over the world based on clues he would send us each week in the form of a handwritten letter (sent to myself via courier or mail or UPS) that I shared with the students. The cities he "hid" in were Chicago, Boston, Montreal, Paris, Rio de Janeiro, Los Angeles, Rome, and Philadelphia.

In the beginning, I didn't tell the students that everything Louie sent us would be in code, so at our first meeting the looks on their faces were priceless. "What does all that mean, Dr. Corley? How are we supposed to figure out what he's trying to tell us?"

I explained that spies, of course, had to code everything they wrote so not just anyone could intercept their transmissions and know things they weren't supposed to know. I was also quick to remind them that Louie knew we were not seasoned spies, so he wouldn't be too hard on us. That was why he limited our search to just eight major cities. Further, he sent us travel guides and maps for all those cities that we could use in our search. That seemed to boost the students' confidence. I also told them that Louie would refer to them as grasshoppers, so when they saw a word with that spelling pattern (two sets of double letters), they were on their way to breaking the code. They were stoked at this point.

We broke the first code (of course we did), then mailed our guess about where Louie was hiding to an address that only I knew. Louie would then let us know the following week if we had succeeded in finding him; that message would be written in a letter using a new code. We would get the city right most often, but we'd always just miss him there. He promised that if we really caught him before he could escape, he would find a way to reveal himself. Onward we went, breaking codes, following his directions, and locating or almost locating him.

One Friday, after we broke the code, Louie's message told us that further clues were waiting for us at Harbor Sweets, a high-end chocolate shop located just a few blocks from our school. The chocolates there are amazing, each of them covered in gold foil, then packed in gold boxes and sealed with a large pressure-sensitive label that covers a lot of the box. After learning that the clue told us to take a trip to Harbor Sweets— an enterprise that also happened to be one of our business partners— the students' reaction was phenomenal.[14] "How are we supposed to get the clues? Is he for real? How does he know about Harbor Sweets?"

I suggested we go there to find the answers. That's what the Friday Club is all about, right? We walked in the shop, then I asked one of the children to tell the clerk that Louie sent us. The clerk appeared to act very surreptitiously, then she carefully handed over a box of chocolates. We returned to school, opened the box, ate some of the chocolates, and found our clues, along with Louie's whereabouts—but again, we had just missed him.

In the midst of all this, I actually lost the codebook, which was stolen from our car when my husband and I dropped off our daughter's belongings in Philadelphia, where she was attending college at the time. When I

---

[14] School business partners are those dedicated to helping local educational institutions. They offer volunteers, donate items, and share their expertise. In this case, Harbor Sweets was also my "partner in crime," having wrapped the box of chocolates and agreeing to play along in our adventure.

met again with the students on the following Friday, I told them the discon-
certing news about the break-in. Most of them didn't believe me. I told them
that I had gotten word to Louie that I was not happy with him, because I
suspected him of stealing the book. He said that he didn't steal it and that it
was far more likely that the culprit was someone who had learned about our
little project and was trying to sabotage it. But the next Friday, I had a new
book of clues, and we picked up where we had left off.

There were a few more weeks to go in our series of spy-hunting meetings. As our time drew to a close, excitement was generated for a big but
unrelated annual event—the fifth-grade overnight field trip. This time
we were going to New York and Montreal. (All of these excursions were
meticulously planned by the aforementioned Kris Wilson, the music
teacher and human Zamboni.)

At our meeting the week before that fifth-grade trip, we broke the code
again and determined that Louie had to be in Montreal. I announced to
the group, "You know what? I'm done with giving Louie enough time to
get away. Since we are actually going to Montreal next week, I'm going
to hold off sending him our answer. I'm going to do it just before we
leave or even on the way there. I think we can catch him!" They were all
in—squared—by then.

We were at the hotel just for one night. The day before, I made
an announcement: any student or adult could attend a meeting the
following evening at the hotel, where important information from Louie
would be revealed. "He's going to make it a little easy on us," I said. "He
gave me a description. He is middle-aged, of medium height, with dark
hair. And he will be wearing a blue scarf." I'm pretty sure a lot of the children did not sleep very much that night.

The next morning, the air was electric. The seventy-five or so of us
from the Saltonstall mingled with the other guests at breakfast, most of
us looking everywhere for a guy with a blue scarf. Eventually, when he
turned the page of his copy of *Le Journal de Montréal*, he revealed his face
and that scarf. There he was for all of us to see: Louie.

I spied him (pardon the pun; I had to do it) just as one of our students in the club, Danny, came up to me, barely able to contain his excitement. "He's *heeeeeeeere!*" Danny whispered to me. "What do we do now?"

I told Danny that I thought he should politely go over to Louie and introduce himself. Likely Louie would offer his name as well. Danny did as I suggested.

Louie folded his paper and replied in broken English, with a thick French-Canadian accent, "Very well. You have caught me." At the end, he smiled, just a bit.

OK, dear reader. Let's pause here. I doubt it's a spoiler for you to read that there is no Louie, and there never was one. All of it was a fantasy, the product of my imagination and some luck along the way.

The man playing Louie was actually the concierge at the hotel, who had graciously agreed to play the role. But the tricky part was protecting him from the insatiable curiosity of a bunch of ten-year-olds eager to hear all about his exploits. This required linguistic acrobatics—that is, the language genius of Perla.

We pretended that Louie spoke primarily French, with an ever-so-slight touch of English, requiring everything to be translated from English to French—by Perla. Actually, I don't believe she translated much of anything the students wanted her to ask him. Of course, she was prepped on everything we had done throughout our spy-hunting weeks, so she could answer any question they had for Louie.

As for the rest of those things? The Harbor Sweets folks were very kind to play along and conceal clues among their Baroque Sarahs and Sweet Sloops chocolates. The car really was burglarized, and Louie's codebook really was taken. As for the arc of the spy-chasing narrative, I just had to roll with it.

Lessons Learned

That particular Friday Club experience was extraordinary, no question. But it was not too far afield from what happened every day in every corner of the giant building at the Salts. It was just the kind of thing we did to make the Saltonstall experience something to write home about. We believed that our students deserved an extraordinary school experience. And providing it made us better educators. So whether it was teaching a new framework for understanding math concepts, a great way to write a narrative, or how to shoot a basketball, we were consistently teaching our students that they could *do* and *be* anything.

All in all, during the five years I was at the Salts, we proved that you can use a shared leadership model to build a strong school culture where pretty much anything is possible. The fact that a college, a school district, and three labor unions could come together to create our break-the-mold school served as a great example for other school districts interested in innovation. And the academic results we achieved proved that our model could work.

For example, in 1997, our scores on state-administered standardized tests were between eight and thirty points higher than the district average in the four core subjects of reading, math, social studies, and science. These high scores continued for our students as they moved on to middle and high school. Moreover, our attendance figures in 1997–98 were 96.8 percent for students and 98.6 percent for teachers, both of which were the highest in the school system. Our attendance at portfolio nights, when students would lead conferences with their parents about what they had accomplished during the term, stood at 98 percent. And almost no one left our school in the years when I was there, unless the family moved out of the area.

My sense of personal satisfaction over what we accomplished at the Salts is enormous. Despite the early setbacks and skepticism (and my own inner doubts at times), everything came together. Just when I thought we'd be making yet another contingency plan, someone picked up the baton or executed some sort of maneuver to make it all work, and on we went. Every time a new obstacle appeared, we found a way through it, with a lot of help from our friends at the district office and city hall. I think we were somehow touched with magic.

Summing it all up, what did I learn?

- Time dedicated to intricate and extended planning is time well spent. It's essential for producing an optimal learning environment, ideal for both students and teachers.
- No matter how much some staff members teased me for my "law-and-order" approach to school culture, it's the only way, in my opinion, to make everything in a school work. (The teasing ceased over time, of course.)
- Teachers deserve a calm environment where interruptions are few.
- A principal's first job is to be a troubleshooter for teachers, keeping unneeded distractions literally and figuratively from the classroom doors.
- When conflicts arise in the classroom, the secret to resolving them lies in the teacher's ability to listen, allowing each and every student to be truly heard. For the students, it's not about stirring up drama but about being acknowledged.
- A core group of top-notch teachers sets the tone for all others. Only the crustiest of "clock punchers" will choose not to join them. Those teachers will ultimately see it our way or transfer to another school or even choose another profession.
- Communication with all stakeholders is to education as oxygen is to the body. With it, the student "body" thrives. Without it, your project, whatever it is, will be on life support.
- The office staff is the backbone of the organization, the force that makes everything run smoothly. The value of office staff members may be less obvious than the value of other staff, but the impact of the office staff is great, and its members must be treated with the utmost respect and care. That also means that having their backs is of prime importance.
- You don't lead to be followed. You lead to grow leaders.

When I look back on my experience at the Salts, I am filled with euphoric recall, a sense of wonder blended with gratitude. When I first got the job, I felt a mixture of excitement and trepidation. But that all turned to joy once we got rolling. What gave me the most satisfaction is that we delivered on our vision. Every promise was fulfilled. Maybe all those eyes focused on us and the pressure that created was a positive, making us work even harder. One thing I knew for sure: the students may have been the ones in the classroom, but every day was an education for me as well as my fellow travelers at the Salts—better than any exotic resort, to be sure.

Moving On

After I left the Salts, I became principal at Bluffton Elementary School in Bluffton, South Carolina. At Bluffton, we were chugging along, making our way up the academic proficiency trail, honing our skills, and focusing our energies on putting the best staff in front of our students. But in 2007, big changes were afoot.

A new superintendent arrived that year and decided that three district administrators and one principal would become academic improvement officers, responsible for increasing academic achievement in each of the four geographical areas of our school district. Unbeknownst to me, I was the lucky principal she had in mind for this job. But two of the three district administrators knew of this plan and arrived one day in advance of the superintendent to warn me.

Mind you, I had always believed, as did my doctoral adviser, that the last best place to affect the arc of students' education is at the building level. I don't mean the literal physical school building: I mean the developmental stage in any school when you're building the educational program. At the time, this was where Bluffton Elementary resided in its evolution. I had zero interest in a "downtown" job since I was already living my dream, and I was far from satisfied with the progress we had made up to that point at Bluffton

Elementary. After eight years, I was not yet finished there. So I didn't take the news about this new job very well.

But two things led me to succumb to the new superintendent's wishes. One was that I'm a company kind of person. If your boss wants you to do a thing, you should do it. The second was something that the two administrators (they were also my friends) shared with me. From what they had heard, it wouldn't be a whole lot of fun to be a principal there anymore, so I might as well join them at the district level.

I served as an academic improvement officer for two years. In the second year, I had the added assignment of overseeing the educational aspects of the construction of two new schools. One was a middle school, and the other was Red Cedar Elementary. The latter is an approximately one-hundred-thousand-square-foot structure that has two stories housing second- through fifth-grade students. On the other end of the structure, there are three "pods" (self-contained areas) with beautifully airy, vaulted, skylit ceilings, each one surrounded by four or six classrooms that comfortably support the work of sixteen teachers and ten assistants and their students. There are forty classrooms with space for what we call related arts (PE, art, music, dance, technology, and a media center), small group teaching areas, and offices. There also is a large and welcoming atrium with a giant skylight.

Red Cedar Elementary is set on an almost block-long lot, bordered on the playground side by thick woods. It sits in a neighborhood of mid-priced single-family homes and some businesses in relatively newly erected buildings. I attended all the construction meetings in the general contractor's trailer, placed across the street from the school, and watched that building rise, making sure there were no change orders, working with district personnel to purchase furniture, reviewing traffic patterns on and around the school campus, approving paint colors, and accompanying various inspectors and the construction supervisor on the obligatory compliance walk-throughs. All these activities involved a lot of the same work as I was engaged in on the Saltonstall project and, many years prior, on a new wing at Heritage Elementary, in Lynchburg.

As we neared completion of the Red Cedar structure, I guess that the superintendent and others noted my enthusiasm for the way the school was coming together. That is, we were hitting all our marks. Construction being a slave to timing, when something or someone does not arrive when needed, it can set the entire schedule awry. But very little of that happened. Fixtures, furniture, building materials—nearly everything fell into place or was forced into it, thanks to an appropriately aggressive building management team from the school district. That provided plenty of fodder for enthusiasm. Things were going well.

The work was very fulfilling, but still, I missed being a principal. I daydreamed not only about being a principal again but about being the principal of Red Cedar. I don't doubt that I let that slip a time or two. After all, for me, being a principal is clearly the best, most rewarding job on the face of the earth. And at the risk of overdoing the superlatives, opening a school is even better than that. In addition, this would be my third opportunity to do so. What more could I ask?

At some point as construction was nearing completion, which coincided with the appropriate time to start the hiring process for the school's leader, the district's chief human resources officer asked if I wanted to apply for the position of principal at Red Cedar Elementary. *Do I want to apply? Well, you bet I do!!*

Another spoiler alert: I got the job. It was incredibly gratifying to be able to see the project through to completion, then open and lead the school in its new home.

But prior to that, as soon as I went through the interview process and secured the position, my mind was racing with possibilities for Red Cedar. Like the stew that had its origins at the Saltonstall, a broad variety of ideas and approaches to teaching and learning were bubbling around in my mind, many of which had been present for use, exploration, and refinement since my days at the Salts. And the greatest opportunity lay in the chance to hire new staff.

A bit of background: when we opened Bluffton Elementary School, a number of teachers were assigned there after the school's attendance zone was redrawn. Some teachers did not want to move. That meant we needed to forge relationships with the staff, establish trust, and agree on a common mission before we could best serve our students. That takes time, energy, and patience. It was quite a different story at the Saltonstall. And this is key: everyone who was at the Saltonstall *wanted* to be at the Saltonstall, both children and adults. It saves a lot of time when everyone can get on the same page quickly, and the positive, collective energy is enormous. So what was the story at Red Cedar?

Since I was a known commodity from my days at Bluffton Elementary, quite a few of the Bluffton Elementary teachers whose goals were the same as mine followed me when I moved there. Further, some of their friends did the same, coming from schools around the district. Then there was the school that I monitored for four months while its principal was out for back surgery. Three of those staff members opted to transfer to Red Cedar as well. In fact, the overwhelming majority of teachers at Red Cedar were like those at the Saltonstall: we were of one mind on the points that really mattered.

That meant that the sky was the limit regarding our potential.

Our approach to culture and climate, determined by our school community (teachers and families), reflected their values, just as they did at the Saltonstall. Teachers at Red Cedar were encouraged to think outside the box, to follow their hearts and notions of best practices in the service of engaging their students and thereby improving levels of teaching and learning. No idea was to be discarded based on lack of funds or time. If it was deemed to be important, we'd find a way to make it happen if at all possible. From the very beginning, careful steps were taken to build bridges with families whose first language was not English, to help them feel that they were an important part of the Red

Cedar community. We wanted to have something for every student to look forward to each day, a reason to want to be there and do their best.

In short, everything I learned in Salem, while it might not have all been put into place at Bluffton Elementary School for one reason or another, found a home at Red Cedar. Chief among them was a culture of enthusiasm, engagement, innovation, pride, caring, and magic.

PART THREE

Responding to Societal Events and Trends

CHAPTER 6

Bullying

Prevention and Response

ONE OF THE MOST DEVASTATING REALITIES OF SCHOOL life is a commonplace form of youth violence in which one student degrades another—verbally, physically, or in other less direct ways. To be considered bullying, this unwanted behavior among school-aged children must be aggressive, involve a real or perceived power imbalance, and be repeated or have the potential to be repeated over time.[15]

It is a treacherously painful thing for any child to experience. According to the National Center for Education Statistics, one out of every five middle and high school students reported being bullied in 2019. The percentage of students being bullied was highest among six, seventh, and eighth graders.[16]

---

[15] For more information, see the US Department of Health and Human Services website on the subject, StopBullying.gov: https://www.stopbullying.gov/bullying/what-is-bullying.

[16] See "Bullying," National Center for Education Statistics, https://nces.ed.gov/fastfacts/display.asp?id=719.

It can happen anywhere—in the classroom, in the cafeteria, on the playground, in a hallway or stairwell, in a locker room, on the bus, in the neighborhood, or on the Internet, whether on social media or via text. In the act of bullying, the bully feels powerful while the bullied child feels powerless, a feeling often accompanied by a deep sense of shame and humiliation. The embarrassment in front of peers can be mortifying.

As I have seen during my forty years of working in schools, bullying comes in four major varieties. First, there is physical bullying, which includes hitting, kicking, punching, pushing, shoving, pinching, choking, and spitting. The bully might also laughingly trip his victim, steal or break his things, or mock him with gestures.

There is also verbal bullying, which includes teasing, name-calling, and insulting as well as taunting, threatening, and making inappropriate sexual comments. I've been spared from the really nasty stuff in the elementary schools I have served, but middle and high school students can be brutal in their condemnations, reaching for the unkindest cuts they can think of from their well-stocked library of pejoratives. Elementary school students imitate negative examples provided by their older siblings, relatives, friends, and sadly, parents. But the intent is the same: to wound with words as much as possible.

In addition, a bully may be indirect. In what is referred to as social bullying, a bully might leave someone out of a group activity on purpose, tell other children not to be friends with that person, spread rumors, or embarrass the victim in public. This includes the ever-popular refrain "I won't be your friend unless…"[17]

Finally, and not least harmful, there is cyberbullying—harassing a student by spreading mean words, lies, and false rumors in chat rooms

[17] The National Association for the Education of Young Children calls this "relational aggression." See Tina Smith-Bonahue, Sondra Smith-Adcock, and Jennifer Harman Ehrentraut, "'I Won't Be Your Friend If You Don't!' Preventing and Responding to Relational Aggression in Preschool Classrooms," *Young Children* 70, no. 1 (March 2015), https://www.naeyc.org/resources/pubs/yc/nov2015/preventing-relational-aggression.

and through emails, text messages, and social media posts. Such electronic bullying may traumatize children without parental knowledge.

In our school, we handled an incident of cyberbullying that occurred when our third-grade teachers set up an online chat room for their ninety students. It was designed to be an academically inclined social forum, monitored by teachers, in which classmates could exchange perfectly benign comments about movies, family trips, soccer teams, books, and progress on assignments. It all worked perfectly until fourth grade began. The chat room was left intact, but there was no adult supervision. It wasn't long before our little friends took advantage of the fact that they were unmonitored. What happened next was disappointing. Around twelve of those students went on a classmate-bashing spree, letting loose with negative and degrading comments about one another. That's when teachers and administrators became involved.

I was disheartened by the students' behavior and confused by it. Why would they use this platform for such a purpose; a narrative shooting gallery of sorts? And how could they carry on with their day-to-day activities and sit next to one another in class after having done something this hurtful?

We met with the bullying students as a whole, in small groups, and as individuals. We had them sit across from one another and read the critical comments they wrote while looking the victims in the eye. Predictably, because they all had at least partially formed consciences, they had trouble doing that.[18]

Afterward, we realized that the students thought *writing* something negative was completely different from *saying* it in person and was therefore basically harmless. A colleague of mine labels this "digital bravery," a

---

[18] Our approach was (and continues to be) restorative justice. It aims to repair wrongs that are committed. It is an appeal-to-one's-better-angels type of technique to get at the root cause of the conflict and to arrive at solutions that will contribute to a positive school culture. The International Institute for Restorative Practices is an excellent source for all things related to acknowledging and mending broken relationships. See https://www.iirp.edu.

phenomenon common in adults as well. The overly emotional, very angry parents who post online criticisms of our school—or of their neighborhood or the post office or their exes—often feel a sense of invincibility, a sense of fearlessness. But they transform into pussycats—with amnesia—when we meet in person to unpack their complaints.

Yes, it was simple enough to shut down the fourth-grade chat room, which we did. But the point was for the students to understand that typing a nasty comment is the same as speaking it, just as a nonverbal gesture is as contemptuous and harmful as a verbal assault. If you're being ugly to someone, no matter how you're doing it (skywriting and interpretive dance included), it's unacceptable and you cannot engage in it. Period.

The Sunny Spot

In our school, one magical spot—an all-glass corner on the second floor that has enough space to seat an entire class of fourth or fifth graders—was dubbed the Sunny Spot by residents of that part of the building when we first moved in. When things are not what they should be—I'm famous for channeling *Star Wars* dialogue and saying things such as, "There's a disturbance in the Force in fifth grade"—I suggest that we all gather in the Sunny Spot and have a talk about the problem and possible ways to overcome it.

Those talks can involve a cast of as many as one hundred people, including students, teachers, counselors, the assistant principal, and a few other central adult figures. Despite the size of the group, these discussions have the vibe of a family conference. The script usually follows a tried-and-true format. I talk about the problem and how it is affecting life among the people involved or the school at large. I explain why the situation is not positive. I explain that it's not "how we do things," and because of all that, it's not sustainable. Staff and teachers add their thoughts to underscore the importance of finding a solution.

The problems include such things as students not listening to teaching assistants, inappropriate bathroom behavior, reckless treatment of others' feelings, and a general decline of decorum. We watch the faces of the students as we speak. Some of those faces seem to say, *Yes! I was hoping you were going to talk about this! But I wouldn't even think about being the one to bring it up.* The seemingly unaffected members of the group might well be perfecting their poker faces because they know we're talking about them; or maybe they just don't care. In either case, we follow up with those students individually.

These conversations in the Sunny Spot make us stronger; they also make us more likely to learn when a child is hurting but not sharing his feelings. We know that visits to the counselor increase after these meetings. Students seem to have more they'd like to discuss. We try to keep it as organic as possible, hoping that we can inspire conversation rather than demand answers—though we do that when necessary. We know that we are getting somewhere when we find that students talk with other students and encourage them to seek adult intervention for their concerns. On a few memorable occasions we brought in featured speakers from the fifth grade who had transgressed in the same way as had the audience members, but they did it a year or two before. In one instance, the fourth graders were getting so competitive during recess soccer that we had to ban the sport for a bit, lest we have too many children on the injured reserve list. Three of the fiercest competitors from that time were now fifth graders who had since become enlightened, qualifying them to convince the fourth graders to take it easy out there on the pitch. My favorite part of their speech was when Ella told the group, "Come on, guys. It's not the World Cup out there. Go half speed. Save the elbows and rough stuff for travel league." She had me convinced. Far more importantly, she had the fourth graders right where we wanted them.

The Broken Windows Theory

In the realm of community policing, law enforcement professionals sometimes talk about the broken windows theory—the concept that each unaddressed problem in a given environment, no matter how small that problem may be, affects people's attitude toward that environment and leads to more problems.

A few "broken windows" can easily metastasize into an extraordinary number of problems if left unaddressed. For example, consider the menace of actual broken windows and graffiti. If this kind of vandalism is commonplace in a neighborhood, the residents get used to it, and an atmosphere of permissibility is established. So even when the rock thrower or spray-painter is caught in the act, he might well offer the excuse "Everybody does it here!"

Bullying is the same. It's a pervasive problem that, when left unattended, can lead to disastrous results for children, families, and communities. We *can't* get used to it. And that's why we, as teachers and administrators, must act quickly and decisively every time a bullying incident comes to our attention. Otherwise, if name-calling, harassing, or belittling behavior is tolerated even once, it sends the message that it's allowable: *I can get away with it. It's what we do around here.* The end result is that more emotional "windows" are broken in the souls of children. And it just keeps happening since the bullied becomes the bully far too often.

Samantha's Story

Keeping a lid on bullying takes constant vigilance and patience. On one occasion, I asked a third grader, Samantha, "Why did you take a swing at Candace on the bus?"

She replied bluntly, "She was mean. And when I don't like what people say, I hit them to make them stop."

What did Candace actually say? As I learned, the extent of her being "mean" to Samantha involved asking where she was from and talking to her about lip balm. Sounds ridiculous, right? But it was enough to provoke Samantha because she felt uncomfortable with those innocent questions.

At our school, the follow-up question to any child who hits another is, "And how does that work for you?" When I asked Samantha this, she defended herself by telling me that she did what she always does. She said that when she and her older sister argue, and she loses her patience or reaches her limit, she simply smacks her sister upside the head to make the whole thing stop. I asked her what happens after that. The answer was, "Nothing."

In other words, there is no parental consequence at home for physical acting out. Nothing gets solved. There is no learning. Mom just yells at both her daughters to shut up, and the behavior is perpetuated. If you're thinking that might not be the truth, in some other circumstances you'd be spot-on. This situation, however, was confirmed with Mom. The child reported the situation at home accurately.

Trust me: if there is little or no parental control, children are going to behave at school exactly the way they behave at home. That's why Samantha simply transferred what she had learned at home to her situation on the bus.

And that's when we knew that we needed to reach out to Samantha's mother to discuss Samantha's dubious conflict-resolution skills. We had to inform Mom of the incident and discuss what does and does not work at school—and in society—by holding up a mirror to the family's way of doing things. But Mom did not want to look in that mirror.

Instead, predictably, she defended her daughter, not realizing that Samantha had conveniently omitted or massaged a few of the details of the incident. For starters, she didn't mention that Candace was two years younger and much smaller than she was. Nor did she mention the lip balm question. But even when presented with these facts, Samantha's mom was resistant to understanding what her daughter had done wrong. Clearly, Mom wasn't going to help the situation.

But we appealed to her better nature: I suggested that we would most definitely appreciate it if the family found a new approach to the sisters', um, "conflict resolution" process. Unfortunately, logic doesn't always work.

Indeed, trying to educate parents is a tricky proposition. They often start out in a defensive posture, or they remain in denial about the inappropriate behavior of their children. Some parents will attempt to minimize just about any unacceptable behavior their children exhibit. As an example, I offer the statement, "But what my son pulled out at the bus stop wasn't a *big* knife." Would that parent really be so forgiving if *her* child had been on the other side of that knife? More on this later.

In any case, when we offer critical feedback, parents often think we are trying to tell them how to raise their children, which they resent. But that's not our intention. Instead, we tell them that their approach to discipline in the home is reflected in what happens at school. And even though allowing physical acting out might work with just two children in a small household, though we have our doubts, it definitely doesn't work in the classroom or on the playground. Such acting out creates a hostile environment that is not conducive to learning, nor is it good preparation for a peaceful life.

Regardless of this logic, some people might minimize bullying and see it as "part of growing up" or "kids being kids."[19] We do not. Just imagine the child who wakes up every morning believing that there is a far better than even chance that he will be met with this abuse—being picked on physically, socially, or through cyberbullying. Should that be part of growing up? It should not.

A Pervasive Problem

Bullying is traumatic to the victim and can have long-lasting consequences. Research indicates that persistent bullying can lead to or worsen feelings of isolation, rejection, exclusion, and despair, which can contribute to suicidal thoughts or behavior. While the vast majority of young people who are bullied do not become suicidal, it can happen.

---

[19] See "Bullying in Schools," Children's Hospital of Philadelphia, https://violence.chop.edu/bullying-schools.

Look no further than a seven-year-old named Jeffery Taylor, who confided to his mom that he was being bullied at school and later shot himself to death. There are many such cases of children and adolescents who have committed suicide because of the torture of being bullied.[20]

There's Rebecca Sedwick, the twelve-year-old who committed suicide in Florida following a year of bullying at the hands of two young girls. To Rebecca, the bullying was so painful she felt that ending her life was the only solution.

There's also the eight-year-old boy who wrote to Santa Claus about his twin sister, who was bullied about her weight: "Dear Santa…I wanted a [remote-control] car and helicopter, but I don't want that anymore. Kids at school are still picking on [my sister] and it's not fair…I prayed that they will stop but god is bisy and needs your help."

Most vivid in my mind recently is the tragic story of Adriana Kuch, the fourteen-year-old in a New Jersey school who was attacked before she died by suicide days later.

Even when bullying doesn't lead to suicide, which it usually does not, such abusive treatment places children at increased risk for depression, anxiety, sleep difficulties, low academic achievement, and chronic health complaints.[21]

Knowing all this, teachers and administrators take bullying very seriously. And we try to get at the core issue: Why would one child bully another?

To the casual observer, it might appear that some students simply have a sadistic streak and take some sort of sick pleasure in asserting their dominance over a person whom they may perceive as weak or

[20] See Donesha Aldridge and Madison Carter, "These Are the Names of about a Dozen Children Who Have Died by Suicide. There Are Thousands More," *11Alive*, updated January 23, 2022, https://www.11alive.com/article/news/special-reports/a-different-cry/children-rising-suicide-death-rates-research-different-cry-series/85-46195650-294b-40a3-97e1-661bbe68a069.

[21] For bullying statistics, see "Bullying, Cyberbullying, & Suicide Statistics," Megan Meier Foundation, https://www.meganmeierfoundation.org/statistics; and "Facts about Bullying," StopBullying.gov, https://www.stopbullying.gov/resources/facts#__Bullying__Research.

defenseless or distasteful or even threatening. True, some children are more aggressive, dominating, and impulsive than others. In my experience, however, that is exceedingly rare.

Other children are neglected by their parents, so they lash out as a way of attracting attention. Their parents might be overwhelmed by challenges or under the influence of drugs or alcohol. They might also be emotionally needy themselves, with little in the tank left for their children. A child who feels aggressive and angry about something at home—something he is powerless to control—may act out that anger toward a fellow student in a way he would never dare to in front of his parents. That child gets a kind of relief from overpowering others.

But bullies don't need a reason to hurt other children. When asked why they do it, some replied,

- Because it makes me feel stronger, smarter, or better than the person I'm bullying.
- Because I'm bullied at home.
- Because it's what you do if you want to hang out with the right crowd.
- Because I see other kids doing it.
- Because I'm jealous of the person I'm bullying.
- Because I'm just so angry.
- Because it's one of the best ways to keep other people from bullying me.

Anyone can become a target, whether you're in elementary, middle, or high school. If you're mixed race or Black, gay or transgender, too short or too tall, too fat or too skinny, too feminine or too masculine, you might become fair game for a bully. It can happen if your clothes are unconventional or you have the wrong hairstyle or struggle with your grades, if you're unathletic or unpopular, if you are "too sensitive," or if you're just plain different.

Sometimes there is no reason at all. Someone may just look like a target who won't fight back. That's enough right there. That's when the bully springs into action.

Moses and Jason

When I was just starting out at Bluffton Elementary, a first grader at our school, who has an African American father and a Caucasian mother, had been called the N-word, not once or twice but multiple times in the course of a few minutes by a fifth grader he did not know. The child, Moses, came home puzzled and asked his mother what the word meant. He was curious about why he was called this. He had no idea. But he sensed that the word was derogatory based on the way in which the other boy said it.

His mother was appalled, both hurt and angry that her son was enduring this abuse. She explained to him that the N-word is a very unkind, mean thing to say—a bad word used to insult and degrade people because of the color of their skin. The boy looked crestfallen and hurt. And he didn't understand it at all. But the mother sure did, and it broke her heart to see her child's innocence tainted by this inexcusable example of hate speech. What to do about it?

In this case, the mother called me and reported the incident. "What," she asked, "is your school policy in a case like this?"

I reacted as I always do when I learn that a child has uttered an awful word or made a demeaning physical gesture. I feel a combination of abhorrence, anger, and shame. After all, I want our school to be a beautiful, welcoming, uplifting place where all humans get along and feel elevated and supported. I don't want any child to observe another one modeling negative or hurtful behavior, then trying it out on fellow students. Or relatives. Or anyone.

Of course, my vision of everyone getting along perfectly at school is idealistic. But I can dream, can't I?

I expressed my displeasure and empathy and my determination to fix things so such behavior will never happen again. In such cases, as I remind our staff, we must make things right with the parent and the child pretty much immediately. I told Moses's mother that I would be talking to both her son and the child who hurt him, then getting back to her after I gathered more information. I also told her that our school counselor would be checking in with Moses that morning.

To be sure, Moses's mom did exactly what she needed to do, what I encourage all parents to do. She put the school on notice that something negative happened to her child and asked how it would be addressed. What she did *not* do was shout at me, blame me for the incident, threaten legal action, or in any way overreact to the situation.

The boy who used the N-word, Jason, had no prior history of aggressive behavior. To the best of our knowledge, there were no other situations in which he used or directed racial slurs at anyone else. Some might say he was a "bully-in-waiting." Nevertheless, there was a power imbalance between the boys as there was a four-year age difference and a four-inch height difference. In Moses's experience, and according to the technical definition, this was bullying behavior. My hope was that because it was Jason's first offense, I could short-circuit future misbehavior through active intervention, which is part of my job, as I see it.

It should be noted that establishing degrees or making distinctions about what is and is not bullying does nothing to make anyone feel better about aggressive behavior, even when an incident is not techni-cally considered bullying. Our administrative handling of that incident does not change. When we learn of such behavior, our school district uses a progressive discipline plan. We consider the age of the child, the severity of the offense, and the number of times it is committed. Age is quite important, because the consequences for a four-year-old are obviously different than those for a high school senior, who has a much higher level of awareness of his own actions and tends to get into significantly more trouble than a prekindergartner.

In any age category, repeat offenders require much more intervention than onetime culprits. As time passes, if a child seems bound and determined to deface school property or talk back to a teacher or physically or verbally abuse other students, we must effectively capture the attention of that perpetrator and do whatever is required to stop him once and for all.

In all cases, we have to determine whether the teacher witnessed the verbal assaults or knew about them. In this case, she did not. We also determined that the action did not occur within range of one of our surveillance cameras. Nor could we find any witnesses. It was one boy's word against another. (Or it could have been.)

Next, we had a conversation with Moses, who was still clearly feeling the sting of that terrible word. He seemed so hurt and sad. And these kinds of talks with students just break my heart. It was clear to me that he was telling the truth.

The following step was to approach Jason, the boy who was repeating the racial slur. He was brought into my office immediately. I had to make him understand how hurtful and hateful using this word was and that he must never do it again.

"Did you call Moses a name that upset him?" I asked Jason.

He haltingly admitted that he had done it.

"You know it was wrong, don't you? You know that there are certain words people say when they want to hurt somebody as much as they can. Maybe this time you didn't mean to say it or didn't understand exactly what you were saying. But it was a terribly mean thing to do, the absolute worst. So now I need to know *why* you did it."

Jason paused for a long time. Sometimes children do that because they're trying to wait out the questioner. And sometimes they just don't know what to say. So I just stared at the boy, which is part of the consequence of misbehavior—that is, putting him on the spot until he takes responsibility for what he did.

Most of the time when a student is stonewalling, I remain quiet during the waiting period. Other times, I might fill in the silence by casually confiding something about myself to the child, such as, "When I've done something that I know is wrong, my stomach reminds me that it doesn't feel very good." I then watch for some kind of reaction from the child. I might ask, "Are you feeling all right? Does your stomach hurt a little?"

If the student says yes, I reinforce the point by telling him that his stomach is reminding him that doing unkind things has a negative impact on more than just the targeted student. It also hurts the person who "shoots the arrow."

In Jason's case, he stayed quiet for at least a minute. And then eventually, as I pressed him for an answer, he said, "I don't know. I just said it." That was all; no reason.

We talked about the fact that the N-word is a very serious word to use. I then asked where he had heard that word in the past. Jason just shrugged his shoulders. I never accept shrugged shoulders as an answer. It is cowardly at worst and deflecting at best.

Sometimes, if a child is old enough to understand the point I'm making, I'll say, "You don't *know*? You don't know why you did it? Are you out of control? You don't know why you do and say the things you do? If that's the case, there's a problem. Because if you're out of control, we can't let you go out to recess or walk through our hallways without someone watching you very, very carefully. Otherwise, someone will get hurt, and you won't know how it happened or why. But I don't think you're out of control. I think you know exactly why you did what you did. You wish you hadn't, but you're not prepared to start making the whole thing right." The youngest of students have an almost cleansing revisionist history approach to this kind of thing. They wish a thing had not happened, so they convince themselves that it just kind of didn't.

Of course, we have to revisit their thinking on that point, because it is what it is.

Jason eventually told me that he had really wanted to *talk* with Moses. But he felt rejected when Moses didn't respond to him in the hallway. *The nerve*, thought Jason. Then Jason and I discussed free will, choices, and the idea that everyone has the right to respond to you or not respond to you, to accept an invitation to play or decline it. As it turned out, Moses did hear Jason say hello and responded with only a half-hearted smile, moving on through the hallway, because he didn't know what to do. Moses had no idea that Jason wanted to get to know him.

After twenty minutes of circling around the issue, I then asked Jason how he thought Moses might be feeling about being called the N-word. I knew I had gotten somewhere because the boy looked me straight in the eye and answered: "Probably the worst day of his life?" Perfectly stated, son.

"So now how do *you* feel?"

Jason kept his head down, eyes glued to the floor. He whispered, "The same for me, I think." Exactly.

Now it was time for him to begin the healing process with Moses—to enable justice to restore a sense of peace. Regarding the consequences: as the principal, I issued Jason a half-day in-school suspension. And I told him that he needed to write a note of apology to Moses, which he immediately did.

Next up was a follow-up discussion with each boy's parents. First, Moses's mother was gratified to know that the school had taken the issue seriously and that there were consequences for the offending boy as a result of his behavior, though we don't talk about the details of those consequences with the other child's parents. She felt good to know that her son would not be the target of any further abuse. I imagine that "good" feeling was guarded; time would tell if what had occurred could be kept from happening again.

Conversations with the offending students' parents are never easy and sometimes involve denial, subterfuge, disbelief, or even blaming the victim or the teacher. But we stick with the facts and focus on what can be learned from the experience. Fortunately, in this case, Jason's parents were apologetic about their son's racist remark and in agreement that the school had handled the issue appropriately.

By the culmination of our disciplinary journey, Jason fully understood that using that hateful word again would constitute disobeying a strict school rule and that he could be expelled for doing so the next time. "Remember, Jason, if you ever use that word again, you will be purposely trying to hurt someone, saying the meanest thing you can think of. That is completely unacceptable, and you now know it."

In my tone, which was calm and even, I didn't shame him, but I did educate him and give him firm rules about what I wasn't going to allow.

In the end, it's not about punishment. Instead, we *appeal to the child's better nature*: "Don't you see that what you did is dangerous for Moses? Can you imagine how hurt and scared he must have felt? You picked the one thing you knew was the harshest you could possibly say. If you were feeling upset with him, there are a hundred adults here to help you with that problem—plus your parents too. But you lashed out and said the nastiest thing you could."

As the school year progressed, Moses and Jason didn't wind up being friends, but there were no further reports of Jason misbehaving. A few weeks after the incident, our counselor facilitated a meeting between the two boys to teach them how to strike up a conversation with someone they'd like to know and how to react if they're on the receiving end of such an overture. That put the train back on the track for both boys.

Skip ahead ten years: one night, at a high school football game, I noticed two very familiar faces on much taller teenage bodies, both of them trombone players in the marching band. They were standing next to each other, chatting and laughing. It was Moses and Jason, now good friends. They immediately recognized me and seemed as happy to see me as I was to see them. I thought, *Music has charms to soothe a savage breast.* Maybe so. It's a happy ending to what began as a cautionary tale.

Daniel's Story

Another disturbing bullying situation came to my attention when one of our bus drivers reported a fight on her route, the bully being a gifted student named Daniel—a fourth grader whose academic performance was negatively affected by a difficult home life. The adverse effects of poverty and desperation were daily realities in Daniel's home. So it was difficult for him and his sister to feel safe and secure there.

The object of Daniel's ire was a perky, super-talkative second grader named Sarah, who tended to be a busybody. Apparently, curious Sarah said one too many annoying things to Daniel while waiting for the bus—nothing derogatory, just repetitions of "What are you doing?" "How come?" and the like. As the bus pulled up, Alice witnessed Daniel punching Sarah repeatedly. She immediately broke up the fight and directed Daniel to sit in the front seat, away from Sarah, as she called her supervisor.

Our assistant principal and I were dumbfounded. We knew things were rough at home for Daniel and his sister (who found the incident amusing). But we had never dealt with anything as remotely serious as this when it came to Daniel. As the assistant principal talked with him, I called his mother to inform her about what had happened. Rather than being shocked by her son's aggressive behavior, she let me have it with both barrels: "You'd better not suspend him for this, because it was not his fault." *Huh?* Mom then threatened to come up to the school and straighten me out. What's more, she planned to bring Grandma (her grandmother) as backup. And so they arrived. Mom was ready for a fight herself. We had a bit of a conversation about the situation, but she maintained that Daniel did nothing wrong and should pay no consequence for anything as I was targeting her son.

Because the assistant principal got pretty much nowhere with Daniel, and I was making no progress with his family members, we switched places in the hope of a better outcome. But before we did that, I announced to Mom that Daniel would be suspended for one day.

When I got to the media center, I found Daniel (who was being supervised by the media specialist) just staring into space. He had been crying and was disinclined to talk to me at all. It seemed to take forever, but I prompted him by saying, "This isn't who you are. So what is this all about?"

He refused to look at me, but he said, "He's out, and she's taking him back," referring to his mother's abusive boyfriend, who had assaulted her several times and had been incarcerated for it. "We were so happy while he was gone," Daniel said sadly, "but now he's back, and they're together again." The emotional chaos this produced for Daniel was incalculable; he had hoped that the chapter with the dangerous boyfriend was closed.

The rage and powerlessness he felt had nowhere to go, so he took it out on little Sarah. This might be understandable but could not go on without serious consequences, which is why we suspended Daniel for the day. Since it was his first offense, this appeared to be an appropriate response.

After that, our team followed up with Daniel closely, supporting him emotionally as much as we could, mostly being there to praise him when he stayed on the right path. A staff member also kept as close tabs as we could on Mom's ups and downs, because Daniel's difficulties had a one-to-one correspondence with hers.

A few years later, when he was in middle school, I was surprised when I got a call from a counselor there saying that Daniel was having a rough day and would speak only to me. Nobody asks his old principal to walk across the parking lot to see him at middle school. No one.

But I stepped in and asked Daniel a few leading questions, starting with, "What can I help you work through, Daniel?" He didn't really say much, so we sat there mostly in silence for twenty minutes. Then once again, I asked, "How would you like me to help you?"

He replied, "You already are." I suppose he meant that I was helping him by just being there, though I felt useless. A short time later, Daniel agreed to speak to the middle school counselor. By both parties' subsequent accounts, they worked out whatever was standing in their way.

Daniel is now an adult with two children of his own. Although his family is not zoned to attend our school, we are in contact from time to time. We've had some pretty serious discussions in the last few years. I am proud that he trusts me and that when we do speak, he is interested in what I have to say.

According to a study conducted at Southern Illinois University in 2018, an estimated 25 to 33 percent of US schoolchildren face some form of bullying.[22] For the longest time, in research literature on the subject, we thought there was just one type of bully: a highly aggressive child who had self-esteem issues that may come from a violent or neglectful home. But that's not always the case.

Sometimes a bully may have originally been a quiet, nonaggressive child who was the target of others' bullying for one reason or another. The point is that if a child is bullied enough, he can transform into a dangerous bully himself.

Children who fall into this category sometimes tend to have better social skills than others and are often charismatic and liked by teachers—a far cry from the "oafish" stereotype of a typical bully. Crucially, these socially dominant children can turn on and off their bullying to

---

22 See Hannah Erickson, "Bullies Often Victims of Bullying Themselves, Research Shows," *SIU News*, September 5, 2018, https://news.siu.edu/2018/09/090518-research-shows-bullies-often-victims-of-bullying.php.

suit their needs and often want to be the leader of the pack. And the way they accomplish that is by pushing other kids down the totem pole.[23]

Much research has been done over the years to understand the correlation between people who have been victims of bullying and people who are perpetrators of bullying. For example, a study conducted by researchers at the Institute of Education in London found that 5 percent of children were bullies, but only 0.5 percent were "true" bullies—those who were not bullied by their peers. That means the remaining 4.5 percent were bullied themselves. The majority (74 percent) of bullies were boys, who suffered the highest levels of depression, anger, paranoia, emotional disaffection, and suicidal behavior.[24]

I think of bullying as a type of contagious virus. And like any virus, if there is no host for it at home, in the neighborhood, or at school, bullying has no place to live and prosper. So it dies.

But if no one stands in the breach between the bully and the bullied, a child may become increasingly angry, hopeless, and vengeful. He might wake up each morning wondering what new and thoughtless hell will be perpetrated on him that day and by whom. It's a horrible feeling, a breeding ground for the desire for payback. Eventually, he will find children he wants to bully in return. In fact, he might think, *Get* them *before they can get* me.

We as teachers and administrators have to be absolutely vigilant about tracking both the bullies and the bullied. Only due diligence makes it possible to derail the cycle of bullying and prevent that rare occurrence of violence that is always brewing in the background. Unless there are policies and people in place to make the bullying stop, the pain continues, and the resentment, hopelessness, and anger fester, leading to potential disaster.

---

[23] See Kelly Oakes, "Why Children Become Bullies at School," *BBC Future*, September 15, 2019, https://www.bbc.com/future/article/20190913-why-some-children-become-merciless-bullies.

[24] See Dan Bloom, "Study Finds Bullies Are the Bullied Too," *The Guardian*, August 29, 2008, https://www.theguardian.com/education/2008/aug/29/bullying.schools.

Cell Phones and Social Media

Since students often use electronic devices to bully other children, I have strong feelings about the availability of cell phones for children between the ages of five and twelve.

To say the least, bullying is an unfortunate misuse of a miraculous machine, one that is indispensable for communication and entertainment. But sadly, some elementary-age children are also using smartphones to share nasty comments, the latest dangerous TikTok challenge, and even nude photos they find on websites they should not be able to access. To be sure, parents need to step up and educate themselves about what their children have on their phones, because all they're doing when they buy cell phones for their kids is handing them the equivalent of a loaded gun. There are parental controls available on those wonderful-terrible devices for a reason.

And that's why I say that cell phones in the hands of children are accidents waiting to happen. They can lead to the exchange of insulting, demeaning gossip and inappropriate text messages that are the very definition of cyberbullying.

There was one incident in which a group of fifth graders was trying to impress one another with how far they could go to disgust themselves, so they sent around all kinds of nasty comments, obscene remarks, and creepy texts. Some of the students were even exchanging adult pornographic photos.

What was most disturbing to me was the evidence that the group was bullying one particular girl. They taunted her by telling her they were going to the movies and that they did not want her to come along. "You won't have anybody to sit with," they texted. "You're fat and ugly, and you say stupid things, which is why nobody wants to be with you."

Wow. Can you imagine how damaging such a text could be to a vulnerable child? It's a sterling and all-too-commonplace example of bullying in action. These phones can become a source of power and pain. A girl treated this way in high school might even have suicidal ideation.

Thankfully, elementary school children don't usually get that far in the emotional cycle of abuse. But if just one child does get that far in that thought process, it's one too many. In any case, these text messages had to stop. They had become so incredibly toxic.

Eventually, one of the parents printed out the texts from his daughter's phone. Outraged, he brought them to the school for us to "do something about it." He complained that besides everything else associated with this hateful behavior, neither he nor his daughter knew everyone in the group. But that was hardly the biggest problem.

As I tell anyone who will listen, giving children a cell phone with totally unrestricted access to the Internet is asking for trouble. Giving children the same freedom regarding who and when and how often to text is just as bad. And the school cannot be blamed for what a child is going to do on that phone, nor can the school manage it. We're overwhelmed with the smorgasbord of responsibilities already crowding our buffet table. Nevertheless, we are happy to help when we can, even though a cell phone has nothing to do with school.

If parents come to us for guidance on the subject, we strongly discourage them from buying cell phones for elementary school students in the first place. Unfortunately, though, we are almost never consulted on the front end of the adventure that is life with children and cell phones. In our view, those devices are just not needed at school. If a child must reach a parent or vice versa, we have a system set up for that. It's very simple. The child tells her teacher that she needs to talk with her parent, and unless there is some nefarious reason for it (not likely), the two are connected by phone as soon as possible.

In fact, we tell parents that no health-care or mental-health agency in the United States worth its federal funding supports the idea of children under age fourteen needing cell phones, which is why I absolutely recommend that parents not indulge a child's insistence that they must have one.[25]

---

[25] See "Why Wait?," *Wait until 8th*, https://www.waituntil8th.org/why-wait.

However, we are not the parents, and we don't make the final decision. And children, the light of their parents' lives, with friends who *all* have the darn things, can be incredibly persistent. If the psychometricians of the state education department really want to see our students' *best* work, they'll title the persuasive essay portion of the standardized exam "Seventy-Five Reasons Why a Child Whose Emotional Intelligence Is Far from Well Developed Should Have a Communications Device That Is Capable of Simultaneously Wreaking Havoc on the Relationships of Each One of That Child's Acquaintances." I would expect that topic to inspire some of the most heartfelt and passionate arguments the students have ever composed.

Still, if parents cave to their children's plaintive cries for a phone, that is their decision. I totally get it. After all, a cell phone is a fun, shiny device that could provide children, as it does adults, a form of instant gratification, fulfilling some of their emotional needs. But it can also be a dangerous gadget.

Let me offer a comparison: if archery sets were popular and children begged for them, can you just imagine if a number of these newly minted archers ran around the neighborhood using one another's backsides for target practice? I think it would be considered absurd and beyond a school's purview to expect its administrators to mediate those disputes. Yet we're in a similar situation with cell phones.

The same thing goes for social media and video games that enable chats. They have age limits on them for a reason, but many parents allow children four or five years younger than those age limits to sign up anyway, even if it means lying about their birth dates.

Above all, the one goal that teachers and parents have in common is the desire to keep children safe. As administrators, we need parents to recognize the dangers within their own homes, especially when they do not use parental controls and when they allow their children to use apps and devices that do not have those controls. For our part, we provide cybersafety education and counseling to our students and parents to help them understand the importance of these safety measures.

All that said, if students insist on bringing cell phones to school, they have to turn them off and leave them in their backpacks. They also need a parent to come in so we can have a conversation about it and they can sign a form that states that they're aware of the rules and the consequences of not following them. No exceptions. Even if students are on the playground or in the cafeteria, they still can't turn the phones on—because they're in their backpacks in the classroom. So what is the point of having one in the first place? Still, some parents feel that for safety reasons, in case of emergency, a child is safer with a phone than without one. So be it.

As long as I'm on the subject of cell phones, let me say something further about them: the usefulness of smartphones in today's world can be overshadowed by their negative effects.

First, staring at an electronic screen takes time away from playing outdoors, hanging out with friends, reading books, and being with family. Face-to-face relationships suffer when children shift their time and energy online, just as is true for many adults. Children sit there dazed, completely in another world.

Second, research shows that for some people, dependence on a smartphone produces the same buzz or high as alcohol, drugs, and gambling do, paving the way for kids to crave these artificial highs and develop other addictions later on.[26]

Third, too much cell phone use is highly distracting and can result in low scores on reasoning and language tests. Some studies even indicate that excessive use of smartphones affects the quality of sleep

[26] See Brian Mastroianni, "Signs Your Child May Have Developed a Smartphone Addiction," *Healthline*, September 22, 2022, https://www.healthline.com/health-news/signs-your-child-may-have-developed-a-smartphone-addiction. See also Sarah Prager, "Cell Phone Addiction and Young Kids: Your Child Is Likely at Risk," *NewFolks*, January 17, 2023, https://www.newfolks.com/inspiration/kids-addicted-to-phones.

children experience and may lead to a premature thinning of the cortex of the brain.[27]

And then there's the fact that kids are not emotionally equipped to navigate social media at an early age. Spending time on Facebook and other sites is exceedingly stimulating, causing the brain to produce a high level of the stress hormone cortisol, which can prevent a child from feeling calm and centered. A student on social media has a constant buzz.

But most important, smartphones put children at risk for cyberbullying. They enable children to view pornography and produce sexual content of their own. Not least worrisome, some apps and social media networks open the door for sexual predators who seek to track children's activity, groom them for sexual trafficking, and interact with them in a sexual way.

I once had a conversation with a child who told me that she felt kind of strange when a person with whom she was playing a game online made a "creepy-looking" avatar that advanced on her avatar. This person's avatar laughed in an odd way, then tackled her avatar and asked, "Was that fun?" I asked the girl who the other player was. Her reply was frightening. "Oh, I don't know. I meet lots of people when I play games. You know, just somebody."

"Just somebody" means it could be anybody! No, she did not tell her mother, because she thought she'd be banned from playing the game if she did. (If Mom is thinking straight, then yes, I hope so.) That prompted a Mom-Dad-counselor-principal sit-down the next day. You see the problems lying in the weeds, I'm sure.

---

[27] See So Yeon Kim et al., "The Relationship between Smartphone Overuse and Sleep in Younger Children: A Prospective Cohort Study," *Journal of Clinical Sleep Medicine* 16, no. 7 (July 15, 2020), https://jcsm.aasm.org/doi/full/10.5664/jcsm.8446. See also Ji-Yeon Yoon, Kyu-Hyoung Jeong, and Heeran J. Cho, "The Effects of Children's Smartphone Addiction on Sleep Duration: The Moderating Effects of Gender and Age," *International Journal of Environmental Research and Public Health* 18, no. 11 (June 2021): 5943, https://www.ncbi.nlm.nih.gov/pmc/articles/PMC8197890.

A Final Word about Bullying

Children must learn that they cannot solve their disputes or ease their frustrations by using ugly words or physical violence. They won't be able to do that as adults in the "real world" without severe consequences, and they can't do it at school either. There can be no confusion about it in the minds of children.

Children—and some adults—need to be taught how to resolve differences peacefully. At our school, we teach students to respect one another and follow the Golden Rule: treat others as you would want to be treated. In my experience, if one student truly respects another, he doesn't risk messing that up with words or actions that might wreck the relationship.

If a student does trample on a classmate's feelings, we have some expectation that the two individuals will deal with the issue appropriately. If not, we intervene and very intentionally teach the steps that can and should be taken to engage in peaceful conflict resolution. You would be amazed at how many children of varying ages have less than a gnat's notion about how this is done.

5 Steps to Conflict Resolution for Children

- **STOP.** Don't let things get out of control.
- **SAY** what the conflict is about.
- **THINK** of positive options.
- **CHOOSE** a positive option that everyone can agree on.
- **RESPECT** the opinions of others, even if you can't agree.[28]

---

[28] See Bob Engler, "Teaching Your Child to Deal with Conflict," Connections Academy, September 2, 2022, https://www.connectionsacademy.com/support/resources/article/building-conflict-resolution-skills-in-children.

Some children—including many who are old enough to know better—can't seem to understand why there would be any conflict at all between themselves and other children because other children should see things their way; their opinions reign supreme. And why do they hold this misconception? No doubt their parents have wittingly or unwittingly conditioned them to think that they are superior beings, entitled to get their way. Such indulged children are often the most difficult to handle because the ideals conveyed to them by their parents create a powerful foundation for belief. And it's difficult to counteract it.

After all, our parents are our first teachers and our premier protectors. They want the best for us and try to set us up with every possible advantage. But what happens when these same people arm their children with ideas that are not acceptable in polite society? What happens when children believe they should get the most attention in the class, have first priority in playing with the cool toys, stand at the head of every line, and be the winner of every contest?

No, it's not OK to push or punch or shove another child into a wall because he got the last copy of a book you wanted from the media center, even if your father told you that you should not take any nonsense from anyone for any reason. The challenge for students like this is learning appropriate boundaries and self-control. They must understand what is socially acceptable and what isn't.

We teach little people—and the big ones too—that *everyone's* opinion has value and that every person is worthy of respect. Using that as a starting point helps derail a lot of the issues that arise when some students believe they are superior to others. But when that belief persists, the "evening up" needs to be explicitly taught.

Our behavior management specialist, Mr. Rod, who also coaches high school baseball, offers some insight into the reasons bullying occurs. "Boys, especially teenage boys, are often not as good at problem-solving as they need to be. They are typically fixated on their cell phones and do not actually talk with one another. They're always texting and are unbelievably distracted. Also, there is more often an instant hostility among boys. It's as if they reach an impasse fairly quickly and are at a loss as to what to do."

I tend to agree with him. Sometimes a student will take your breath away, pitching a fit like a toddler over seemingly nothing—a friend not passing the soccer ball to him or declining an invitation to work on a project. I think, *How could you possibly get so worked up over something this trivial?* But these are children who view everything as vitally important.

We teachers and administrators must teach the conflict-resolution skills that are crucial to building a foundation of mutual respect. Over and over, we must drill into students that not everything can go their way. Instead of total capitulation on the one hand, or war on the other, there can be compromise. It is important for us all to make space in our psyches for opposing opinions, listening to others, and becoming more empathetic, all of which are the hallmarks of a maturing mind. And the earlier children learn this, the better.

Remember the theory about graffiti and broken windows? Once the destruction begins, we risk it becoming the norm. It works the other way too. You can have unbroken glass, clean walls, and respectful children—and adults—if you settle for nothing less.

Helping to Stop Bullying

We have an app called *See Something Say Something*, which does just what you think it would. Anyone, whether adult or child, who is looking for assistance in dealing with bullying or circumstances resembling bullying can use it. The message is sent to the highest officials in the district and the head of counselors. In turn, our counselor, social worker, behavior management specialist, assistant principal, and principal are notified. We respond to acknowledge that we have received the complaint, resolve it through investigation, implement restorative justice, and assign consequences if appropriate. Then we follow up with a short statement about our actions. This has proven to be a most effective tool.

CHAPTER 7

COVID-19

Flying Blind into a Storm

IN 2020, AS OUR SECOND SEMESTER AT RED CEDAR Elementary was about to begin, we were enjoying typical South Carolina January weather, cloudy and in the fifties.

On schedule, full school buses arrived, accompanied by a long line of cars that snaked around the block as the parents who chose to drive their children to school waited to drop them off. After two weeks of vacation, our army of six hundred students was returning to the classroom refreshed, many of them bubbling over about all the things they had done during the holiday break. As the doors opened and students poured in, the hallways buzzed with the typical chatter about who had gotten what for Christmas and who was playing the latest video games.

In preparation for their return, our administrative and custodial crew had gotten the facilities all cleaned up and ready to go, while our teaching staff had its usual pre-semester planning meetings. We were fully staffed and prepared not only for the what, when, and how of teaching the curriculum before us but also for all fourteen of our before-school and after-school programs. It was all systems go.

During the first two and a half months of that semester, we rolled along with no snags—hosting our monthly School Improvement Council meetings, getting together weekly in our Professional Learning Communities,[29] rehearsing and performing the musical programs, hosting a visit from the Hilton Head Symphony Orchestra, staging a math competition called Battle of the Bluff (the derivation of the name of our town, Bluffton), taking class pictures, and putting on a well-attended Family Valentine's Dance, where entire families were dressed in red and pink outfits (or plaid—there was lots of plaid that year) and ate food fit for the occasion. We also started the mandatory round of second-grade swimming lessons and participated in March Book Madness. Everything about the semester was well planned and executed.

And then on Sunday, March 15, 2020—bam! Everything changed.

Before that day, SARS-CoV-2, termed COVID-19, had already been in the news. The first mention of it was in early January. But because the disease was initially limited to China, the threat seemed distant. Even when the first case of the virus reared its ugly head in the United States, we figured South Carolina is quite a few fuel-and-food stops away from Seattle, Washington. We thought for a while we might be in the clear. Life at our school hummed along as usual: classwork continued, the staff held its meetings, and the students engaged in their daily routines, unaware that their lives would soon change forever.

By mid-February, of course, news of the contagion had ramped up. More cases were being reported outside of China as the respiratory infection extended its tentacles westward. China itself began to take drastic

---

[29] Rick DuFour is the father of professional learning communities. He says that there are four critical questions to ask in PLCs: (1) What do we want all students to know and be able to do? (2) How will we know if they learn it? (3) How will we respond when some students do not learn? (4) How will we extend the learning for students who are already proficient?

measures by tearing down buildings, locking down entire cities, and constructing a new hospital just to treat patients who had the disease. Some of us started to wonder and worry. Something was up.

Having already breached the United States, COVID-19 started to spread like wildfire. In March, reports came in about infections in New York City, New Orleans, and other major American cities as well as throughout Europe. Worse still, these reports told of infections that resulted in hospitalization and ended in death.

The mounting bad news prompted us to prepare homework materials in the event that our students were prohibited from coming to school. We were operating on hunches, not facts, but still, the laptops went home with the students that Friday.[30] The homework packets, however, were delayed because the task of compiling them was so labor-intensive and time-consuming. It was clear that we would have to figure out how to make the new learning pipeline work and that it would take some effort and patience as well as some dedicated personnel and advanced logistics.

Our fourth and fifth graders typically took their laptops home each day to complete classwork, read via e-books, and work on math tutorials. Third graders generally did not take their computers home, and second graders had never done so. Because we had anticipated that some sort of school-closure order might be imminent, we especially needed to prepare the students and teachers at the second-grade level for what might happen. The children needed to know how to care for their laptops appropriately. That included how to log in from home, how to charge the laptops, and a laundry list of what *not* to do away from our teachers' watchful eyes. So the laptops were sent home accompanied by supportive instructions for parents to assist in case we were going to be virtual at some time in the future. On

---

[30] Students at Red Cedar use laptops provided by and owned by the school district. These laptops are tightly controlled: the children can't get on the "regular" Internet with them—only our sanitized and controlled version of it.

Friday, March 13—the date seemed particularly ominous—we were preparing for the worst, even though there was no government order in place yet to cease in-classroom instruction.

Indeed, that Friday, once we made it to the afternoon with no word from the governor's office, everyone assumed we would all be back together as usual on Monday. But that was not to be.

We did not go back on Monday.

In fact, we didn't go back to school that entire year.

We never got to tell our students in person, in the cocoon and warmth of our classrooms, how we were going to work things out and finish the year remotely. Nor did we have the opportunity to be emotionally supportive, telling the children in all those classes that they were going to be OK. We had no chance to prepare them for what lay ahead.

We never got to say goodbye at all.

On Sunday, March 15, 2020, South Carolina's governor, Henry McMaster, issued an executive order calling for the temporary closure of all public schools in addition to all state colleges and universities. COVID-19 had to be stopped, and closing the schools was part of the overall effort.

In all my years as a principal, nothing like that had ever happened. It was new territory for all school administrators, none of whom knew quite what to do.

Initially, schools were left to navigate their own way forward. To me, the responsibilities ahead amounted to nothing short of a military operation—keep calm, forge ahead, "Nothing to see here; we're just learning in a different way." Our new reality would become remote learning, a complex dance involving computer technology, administrative supervision, and classroom materials, all of which allowed us to maintain some continuity—once we adjusted.

On Monday, March 16, staff began to set up makeshift classrooms for online learning in their own homes. Naturally, many of our teachers had their own children to get settled into their at-home school routines as well. They had to acclimate, motivate, and engage students, all while keeping their own children on track.

Parents who were able to work remotely faced similar challenges: getting their children to do schoolwork while they also worked. Parents who had to leave the house scrambled to find babysitters, often relatives who could pinch-hit. But none of it was easy for anyone.

The mission was to deliver basic educational tools to each child and family who needed them. Sometimes people picked up the materials; sometimes we delivered them. Our deliveries included some 280-plus packets of classwork, along with paper, crayons, pencils, counting aids, and any other necessary classroom items.

Before COVID, our kindergartners and first graders had iPads assigned to them, but they were only usable at school and not technically operable from home. So those students worked on paper.

Even though our second through fifth graders were pretty facile with anything that showed up on their screens, often completing assignments on Google Classroom and a variety of other educational software, they were not yet prepared to use Zoom for videoconferencing. The adults were in the same boat, most of them having only heard of Zoom for the first time at the end of the prior week. Our team, however, felt we could overcome that hurdle quickly. And indeed, as time passed, though it took some getting used to, both teachers and students adjusted and became quite adept at handling classwork, retrieving assignments, completing them at home, and yes, even using Zoom.

First and foremost, remote learning meant that all our students had to have Internet access at home. That was a given. No Internet—and no Wi-Fi—meant no learning. Unfortunately, the economically disadvantaged children sometimes lacked this modern convenience in their home. So the pandemic exacerbated the preexisting inequality among students, causing the disadvantaged kids to be handicapped academically. Our team knew that could not stand.

My belief is that education is supposed to be the great equalizer and that all students should be able to do whatever they want in life if they have the will and training to do it. But if learning is compromised by the absence of the Internet and other vital tools, then those underserved children are definitely cut out of the loop, when they need to be present in every sense of the word.

To help assure that no family missed the digital boat, Mr. Mullins, a supporter of our school who worked at a communications company, made sure that Wi-Fi was set up and running for *all* our students. Later on, when we returned to "in-person" school, he kindly brought scads of disinfectant wipes and hand sanitizer to the classrooms.

In addition, an excellent use of courtesy discounts thanks to Mr. Mullins, along with a few dollars from me, ultimately secured Internet access for all our families. Later, the South Carolina Department of Education and our school district provided Wi-Fi hotspots as well.

Beyond the academic issues related to working remotely, there were other equally important practical concerns as we adjusted to COVID-19 times. First, our students needed to eat. Because many of them depended on meals at school, we needed to make certain that those who participated in the National School Lunch Program and the School Breakfast Program kept getting fed. That program soon became free for all students throughout the country and remained that way for a year after we came back to school. Opinion: That was a massively spot-on thing to do regardless of family income under these circumstances.

I spoke with our contact at Sodexo, our student meal supplier at the time, and we devised a plan for distributing breakfast and lunch at the school. Of course, not everyone was able to stop by, and even some of those who did soon had to quit coming because they couldn't afford the gasoline for their cars, whether as a result of reduced work hours or total job loss. In response, Mr. Rod and others drove many miles through our area's neediest neighborhoods to distribute meals. He knew that this was also an opportunity to check in on the students most at risk of falling behind—or worse, with their families, falling off the grid. Over time, our transportation folks helped out as well by running a few bus routes to drop off food. We advertised the heck out of the stop times, and families responded by turning out in droves.

We also did what we could to keep other programs running. For example, Backpack Buddies has always been part of life at our school.[31] Volunteers from churches and synagogues pack bags of snacks that go home on Fridays with students who need them. After the lockdown began, they continued to do this on a wider scale, covering most of the schools in Bluffton.

Early on during the pandemic, we assembled a team we dubbed the Front Line, staffed with nonteaching professionals who could troubleshoot computer and Wi-Fi issues. This squad routinely helped talk parents off the ledge—sometimes using their children as translators (interpreting technological terms and toggling between English and Spanish). Typical technical issues involved ClassTag, our parent-teacher communication vehicle; Google Classroom; Zoom; Wi-Fi; and ClassLink, the one-stop interface for all district-sponsored software. Nontechnical issues involved students and their families getting used to the new normal, a normal that no longer allowed a student to walk up to a teacher for assistance.

In short, dealing with COVID issues nonstop had become a full-time job on top of the jobs we already had. It was a frenetic time, to say the least. Granted, the South Carolina Department of Health and

---

[31] Backpack Buddies is a loose association of local groups that are run independently. The various groups share information about how to make deals with local food banks and other sources. They share information about recruiting volunteers and working with schools and distribution methods too. Most of the schools in our district welcome their help. A few dedicated heroes are in charge of the acquisition of the food, and they get others to work with their churches and synagogues to make the magic happen. Our social worker identifies the students who will receive the food and communicates with parents for permission to send it home with the students.

Environmental Control, along with our school district, provided some guidance on how to move forward, but that's all it was. Missing were firm directives. We were all flying blind together in a dangerous storm, and it was clear that this virus might result in more than just respiratory casualties.

To be clear, Beaufort County School District leadership engaged all of its resources to absorb, discuss, and disseminate guidance for dealing with the pandemic with principals and department directors. We had many questions, most of which could not possibly have been anticipated. That meant setting up a help system (like we had done at the school level for families dealing with the same types of things at their level). It probably goes without saying that more than a bit of that "guidance" was met with derision by parents. We, at the school level, were the natural targets; just a side benefit to our new normal.

As everyone who survived the pandemic can recall, guidance on the national and international level was ever-evolving, which was read as inconsistent at best and flat-out wrongheaded at worst. The Centers for Disease Control and Prevention, the World Health Organization, and the White House sent mixed messages, if they sent any messages at all. At first, face masks were recommended for frontline caregivers only. And then, after some time, everyone was told to wear them. Social distancing was mandated, but experts disagreed on how many feet apart people should stay. Almost overnight, plexiglass shields appeared in grocery stores and at many retail locations in a desperate attempt to minimize the spread of the virus. And yet some people argued that such measures amounted to little more than hygiene theater. When vaccines finally arrived on the scene, their use was hotly debated, and many people made wild, unfounded claims about them. Social media became the forum where anyone with an opinion could spread useful information as well as misinformation.

All during the pandemic, my primary concern was for the health and safety of our students and staff. And I was constantly asking myself if we were missing some measure that would prevent COVID-19 from spreading inside our school. As for my own health, I wasn't that worried. However, I was concerned about bringing COVID-19 home to my husband, Wayne, so I tried to do everything right.

Being hypervigilant, we realized that we could do nothing about protecting staff and students outside of school—they could socialize as they pleased. In fact, a few students' families informed us that they planned to go on vacation during the lockdown and requested particulars about ways to connect for lessons from their hotel rooms. Our answer was that attempting to "remote in" from a hotel or other vacation spot was not acceptable. If that happened, we would count their children absent. Case closed. Except for some rare exceptions, our school district developed a policy that prohibited the use of our computers once they left the state.

Red Cedar Elementary School COVID-19 Timeline

- Early March 2020: Governor McMaster issues his mandate, closing all schools; virtual learning commences for all students.
- Summer 2020: Virtual learning stays in place during summer school.
- Fall 2020: School opens, still fully virtual.
- October 5, 2020: A hybrid schedule is put in place, with two days of in-person learning and three days of at-home learning per week.
- January 4, 2021: A fully in-person schedule is instituted for any student who wants to return to face-to-face learning; around 80 percent of the students at our school return. These numbers vary widely from school to school across our district.
- Fall 2021: Governor McMaster lifts the mask mandate; subsequently, 30–40 percent of students still wear masks, but that number steadily dwindles.

Throughout the pandemic, Red Cedar's infection rate among students remained consistently low, even after the governor lifted the mask mandate in the fall of 2021. But in January of 2022, the infection rate among both students and staff suddenly rose. This might have been attributable partly to the Christmas break as well as to the insurgence of a new, more contagious variant. In fact, during that month's COVID-19 spike, so many staff members throughout our district were in quarantine or isolation that many of our schools had trouble fielding a full roster of employees each day. Our school was no different.

During that time, we taught using dual modalities. This meant that a teacher might instruct all day in person with some of her students in class and others participating on Zoom. Alternatively, a teacher might need to teach from home while some of her students were also at home and some of her students were present in class. In those cases, we would have an assistant in the classroom to tend to the students' physical and emotional needs and supervise the class. The students at home would view lessons on their laptops, and those in class would view lessons on the teacher's presentation board. It was a challenge, but we made it work.

Once our children were learning remotely, we found around fifteen different ways to enhance a lesson electronically. From Flipgrid (now known simply as Flip) to something called Gizmos (from ExploreLearning), we used every application we could find to complement lessons and capture the students' attention, because that was the key objective. Flip, for instance, is a video tool that helped us facilitate discussions across multiple digital devices and even allowed more reticent students to record their responses to questions numerous times before they felt confident about posting them, while Gizmos gave us access to a seemingly endless supply of engaging math and science simulations.

Some of these digital applications came in handy in other ways. When you're teaching children, you practice something called proximity control. For example, if you walk over to Jonathan while he's cutting up with his friend Sam, he'll likely stop (unless he has some other compelling reason to call attention to himself). Of course, when your entire class is on Zoom, you can't do that. But with some of these applications, you can send a direct message like, "Hey, Jonathan!" to a student and refocus his attention without losing the attention of the rest of the class.

We also used anything that was similar to Google Classroom, including Seesaw. Seesaw and Google Classroom are alike in that they both act as storehouses for lesson videos and other information, such as homework assignments. What's more, we used something called Padlet to help the teachers communicate with students and parents. It enables users to collaborate in real time and for all types of media to be posted too.

The program Kahoot! was also a big help because it allowed teachers to create a quiz with music in the background. When students hear the music, the teacher says, "Yep, we're doing a Kahoot!," a short, multiple-choice quiz, typically ten questions long, during which students try to give the correct answers as fast as they can. Kahoot! has a leaderboard where scores are displayed for everybody to see. It can be used in person or remotely. And the children love the interactive and competitive nature of it.

Quite a few of these applications had been used during in-person learning (a.k.a. synchronous learning), but they became indispensable during remote learning (a.k.a. asynchronous learning) because they allowed for the prepared lessons to be consumed at whatever time worked best for the family.

As effective as all these electronic learning tools were in adapting to our new circumstances, they also posed a tough and rather unpleasant challenge—a new variety of behavioral issues. For example, errant children would purposely manipulate a program on the computer and then claim that the laptop or the software was not working. And sometimes we had to go to extraordinary lengths to convince parents that their children had not submitted their homework when the parents swore

they had. Thankfully, the Beaufort County School District tech department stepped in to help, allowing us to prove whether this was the case.
Beyond the district's assistance (I am not at liberty to divulge sources and
methods), teachers could also take a screenshot of what was submitted,
complete with a time-and-date stamp.

In addition, the iboss security software sent me a report each
morning that raised a red flag whenever a child visited a banned site or
performed a prohibited search. If I found anything troubling, I sent it
to our behavior management specialist with suggestions about how to
handle it. Our teachers also had access to Dyknow, which allows them to
see, in real time, each of their students' screens. In addition, we used a
utility called Gaggle, which alerted us by email whenever students wrote
direct or implied injurious statements about themselves or their classmates. We continue to use all these programs today.

This leads to the point that the pandemic and lockdown created
mental health challenges for children. Despondence, worry, and a sense
of disorientation were at an all-time high. Some children were confused,
afraid, and lonely, while a few viewed the break from school as fun,
an excuse to be lazy. Our littlest ones, who often need their teachers
emotionally more than the older students do, appeared to be affected
the most.

One study conducted in Argentina in July of 2021 found that two
months of pandemic lockdown there "affected [the] emotional state and
lifestyle of children and parents." It further observed that "during the
COVID-19 crisis, strong links [existed] between parental psychological
status and the well-being of children." The study also found that "lockdown especially affected the emotional well-being of more vulnerable
families."[32]

---

[32] See Maria Victoria Fasano et al., "Consequences of Lockdown during COVID-19 Pandemic in
   Lifestyle and Emotional State of Children in Argentina," *Frontiers in Pediatrics* 9 (2021), https://
   www.frontiersin.org/articles/10.3389/fped.2021.660033/full.

Another study found high rates of increased irritability and increased laziness in four- to ten-year-olds during the pandemic, a finding our teachers would support.[33] Still another study surveyed mothers who reported an increase in emotional symptoms, behavior problems, and hyperactivity and inattention issues in their children during the pandemic.[34]

Of course, there are very real reasons for all this mental anguish. Just in our little world at Red Cedar, tragically, three student families lost one of their parents to the virus, and one family lost both parents approximately a year apart. Other parents became quite ill but eventually recovered. Imagine being a child with a seriously ill parent while having your entire world disrupted at school by a pandemic. We won't know for years how all this has affected the psyches and emotional development of the world's children.

Beyond the children who lost a parent to COVID-19, we've had many more lose extended family members, such as great-grandmothers, who might have lived some distance away. At the time I write this, I think it would be hard for me to walk down the school hallway and find twenty students who have not been affected by COVID-19. Through it all, though, our teachers stood tall and tended to their student flock as best they could.

Naturally, the pandemic and the lockdown affected children's academic performance too. As a whole, grades slipped some, but we did what we could to apply grace at every opportunity, giving the children more leeway than usual on assignments and tests. Now that the pandemic is in our rearview mirror, striking the balance between grace

---

33 See Josefine Rothe et al., "Changes in Emotions and Worries during the COVID-19 Pandemic: An Online-Survey with Children and Adults with and without Mental Health Conditions," *Child and Adolescent Psychiatry and Mental Health* 15, no. 11 (2021), https://capmh.biomedcentral.com/articles/10.1186/s13034-021-00363-9.

34 See Gemma Sicouri et al., "Mental Health Symptoms in Children and Adolescents during COVID-19 in Australia," *Australian and New Zealand Journal of Psychiatry* 57, no. 2 (2022), https://journals.sagepub.com/doi/full/10.1177/00048674221090174.

and rigor in the arena of performance expectations remains a delicate juxtaposition. We need to make up for lost time. We also need to give students the same thing—time to ramp back up and do their best work.

When students finally did come back into the physical classroom, their reactions varied depending on their grade level. Our third-grade, fourth-grade, and fifth-grade students in particular were thrilled to be back because they remembered what they had been missing.

But when our younger students returned, they weren't as sure about what to do, especially since they had left right as they were getting into the scholastic routine. Our second graders that year had a certain kindergarten quality to them. Why? Because kindergarten was the last time they were in school for a full year. And our first graders that year had not been in school at all until the student body returned.

Through this entire ordeal, our counselor and social worker did everything they could to support our staff, who had to teach in this "new normal" while keeping track of their own families' health. It was a monumental challenge.

Our school nurse, Bethany Byrne, was an angel on earth, the rock of our organization. But as stable and clear-eyed as she always had been, her burden went from difficult to barely manageable.

Her first priority was student health and safety. Typically, before the pandemic, sick children would go to her office for care. If someone called her on our two-way radios to say that a student needed a temperature check and that the student was coming down to see her, she would acknowledge the call and wait for the child. But during the pandemic, there were new protocols. If a student walked down to the nurse's office, he might encounter other children in the hallway, potentially infecting them too. The student would wait in an office adjacent to their classroom and Nurse Byrne would make "house calls" instead.

Her job was not only becoming more labor-intensive but also expanded to include contact tracing, a huge challenge. A parent would call Nurse Byrne to say that someone in the household had contracted COVID-19. She would then record the information and ask questions about who might have been in close contact with that person or need to be quarantined. Always empathetic and a great listener, Nurse Byrne had to cope with the emotional reactions of somewhat freaked-out teachers while managing frightened parents, explaining the infection's symptoms and how best to recover. You can imagine that these exchanges were quite time-consuming and elicited a surprising variety of responses from parents. Some were deeply worried and fearful, while others were quite cavalier. Some angrily debated with her. Or, I should say, they *attempted* to do that. She didn't take the debate bait.

Through it all, Nurse Byrne was absolutely fantastic, and it was her emotional stability that helped us keep a steady hand on a constantly changing situation. For example, she remained calm whenever a flurry of medical updates was handed down from the government to our school district like stone tablets—albeit tablets made of really soft, porous stone. First, quarantines and isolations were to last for fourteen days, then ten, then five. Each time the length changed, Nurse Byrne explained what that meant and the possible rationale behind the change, then comforted the people who went from quietly listening to catastrophizing the new information.

In addition, parents' views of us changed over time: at the beginning of the pandemic, we were gods and goddesses, to be adored. Some parents even placed signs on our lawns that said, AN EDUCATION HERO LIVES HERE. But sadly, that didn't last. More than a few critical parents viewed us as lazy and afraid when some teachers on a national forum expressed consternation about returning to in-person teaching and learning. I found all of it somewhat anxiety-provoking myself. I had never been in a circumstance where you could make so many people so unhappy just by following government mandates, nor had I been in a situation where such strong feelings from parents existed on every point of the spectrum.

When it came to vaccinating children, there were many anti-vax folks in our state who were dead set against it. Mind you, we didn't suggest vaccination or request that anyone receive the vaccine. That was not our call. But that did not stop some parents from offering their unsolicited opinions about vaccinations and COVID-19 testing in general. The saddest of those was the parent who said she *knew* that the swab for collecting samples was contaminated and actually *caused* the virus. After a long hospital stay, she was one of the parents who was lost.

When the government said that it was safe for children to be vaccinated, we never knew how many students did or didn't get the vaccine, because that information is private under federal FERPA rules. We were basically working in the dark.

Once our school partially reopened, in the fall of 2020, we employed a number of safety and sanitation measures to fight the spread of COVID-19. We required masks; we cleaned and sanitized surfaces; and we installed plexiglass barriers in certain locations. We didn't know whether those methods worked—no one did at the time—but we were vigilant about trying to keep our school clean and safe.

The school district's protocols also required that children wear masks not only in school but also on the bus. In fact, the district used portable sanitization systems on the buses that sprayed the interiors with a disinfectant mist. In addition, whereas other schools spaced student desks farther apart than they had been, that option wasn't open to us, because our students sit at long tables, a seating arrangement we find more collegial. Still, although we used to seat two children at each 6-by-2.5-foot table, we then sat only one. It was a little lonely for the students, but safer.

In addition to adjusting the classroom seating, we minimized the time students had to spend waiting in line. Lunch was delivered to the classrooms, and music, art, and technology classes were held in students' "home" classrooms, with the teachers of those subjects coming to the students instead of vice versa. PE and dance still carried on as before but with more physical distance among students. And to encourage social distancing, we placed little fox stickers on the floor, six feet apart, in places where children tended to line up for activities. As the students stood in line, their teachers would say, "Are you on a fox?"

"No, but I'll get there," a child might reply.

And of course, you still can't go twenty feet in our building without encountering a hand-sanitizer pump. They remain today because there is no reason to remove them. Some children are so conditioned to use them that they'll readily inform us if we run out of what a few of our youngest call *hanitizer*.

Despite all our meticulous precautions, there were the parents I called the nonbelievers, those who defied any rules. Admittedly, of the 1,200 or so parents of students at our school, only a handful were obstructive nonbelievers. But they did get under my skin.

One mother came in to complain about our continuing with virtual learning. Her strident voice only made the discussion that much more unpleasant as I tried to explain our position to her. She first thought that our mask mandate was silly. And then she wondered why we couldn't do what grocery stores were doing, which was to let everyone and anyone in without any consideration of how crowded the store might be.

I said to her, "Here's the part that you're not getting. I am responsible for the well-being of everybody who crosses the threshold of this school. A grocery store, on the other hand, is not responsible for its customers' health. They're only liable if a customer slips on a wet floor." I went on to explain that we all felt deeply responsible for preventing any child from contracting COVID-19, taking every precaution we could and enforcing the mandates handed down by the governor, the South Carolina Department of Health and Environmental Control, and the school board.

Sadly, I didn't succeed in protecting all students from infection. Nobody could. From March of 2020 until the spring of 2022, some 30 percent of our student body did catch the virus. And along the way, we had to temporarily close a few classrooms, though our school never closed down once it had reopened. And most important, no child died from COVID-19 at Red Cedar.

While my entire focus as a principal was to prevent staff and students from infection, I was not immune to it myself. In early 2022, both my husband and I contracted COVID-19. But luckily for us, we each had a mild case akin to a severe sinus infection, although we did experience its attendant fatigue.

Several of our teachers, too, became ill, although fortunately that was the extent of it. Still, they felt the increased stress of having to deal with the strict protocols and safety measures, all while worrying about bringing COVID-19 home or bringing it from home to school.

Not surprisingly, teacher burnout was common throughout those pandemic times, raising concerns about a potential increase in teacher turnover and future teacher shortages. In a RAND Corporation survey conducted in January and February 2021, nearly one-quarter of teachers surveyed indicated a desire to leave their jobs.[35] Indeed, many teachers across the country retired because they believed that school was an unsafe work environment. Another survey, conducted by the National Education Association, found that a full 55 percent of educators across the United States were "planning to leave the profession or retire early."[36]

But I didn't feel the impulse to abandon ship. Not at all. Instead, as a senior principal, I became a go-to person for community information. Our school superintendent, local news reporters, and others often asked

---

[35] See Elizabeth D. Steiner and Ashley Woo, "Job-Related Stress Threatens the Teacher Supply," RAND Corporation, https://www.rand.org/pubs/research_reports/RRA1108-1.html.

[36] See Patrick Phillips, "55% of Teachers Planning to Leave Teaching or Retire Early, Survey Finds," Live 5 News, updated February 1, 2022, https://www.live5news.com/2022/02/01/new-survey-examines-teacher-burnout-impact-educator-shortage.

my advice and opinion about protocols and procedures. And I asked *them* to give the school principals and nurses a heads-up whenever a new protocol was introduced.

The entire COVID-19 crisis demanded the ability to adapt and remain flexible. But despite whatever was thrown at our staff, I felt confident that we could handle it. Remember Ross, a character from the television show *Friends*? He used the word *pivot* a lot. That was the motto on our staff shirts that year. It sure fit the times.

So what have I learned from all this? First, as educators, we have to be prepared to turn on a dime when we're confronted by the unexpected. We need to bob and weave adeptly to get ahead of impending health threats. In the case of COVID-19, the second a new finding or mandate was released by the district office, I always digested it immediately and sent the information to our school nurse, then to the rest of our leadership team.

In addition, I've always been good at getting people to "pick up a rake in the yard," as I like to say. You know, if you step on a rake that you can't see in the tall grass, it can swing upward and whack you in the face. So if you know there's a rake out there, pick it up now to prevent an accident later. And if you know a threatening situation is looming, do what you can to get ahead of it.

But more than the importance of efficient administration, the experience confirmed my thinking about the importance of teamwork—the need to assemble a strong, inspired staff who can handle this kind of threat and others. The pandemic and the initial lockdown were jarring partly because they were so sudden. I never would have thought that the time we spent together on that Friday before our school closed would be the last in-person session for the rest of the school year.

But our strong, inspired staff had always been prepared to "do the next important thing." And although the speed at which we needed to react, check our own misgivings and concerns, and prepare the best educational program for our students made it a monumental task, we did it. In fact, we did it well. Were we sure we could pull it off? Not so much.

As I write this chapter about my pandemic experience, my heart aches for the families of the more than one million people in the United States who died of COVID-19, including some thirteen thousand children. We must protect our children and ourselves in any and all ways we can. And my role as a principal is to be a fierce protector of and safety net for anyone in our school who needs it.

CHAPTER 8

Gun Violence

Here's the Drill

IN JUNE 2022, TWO WEEKS AFTER NINETEEN CHILDREN WERE killed at an elementary school in Uvalde, Texas, Oscar-winning actor Matthew McConaughey stood behind the podium in the White House Briefing Room. He was both incensed and heartbroken as he delivered a powerful speech about the desperate need for gun control in America.

That day, as I sat in my office watching the speech on television, I was gripped by his comments. "We need to invest in mental health care, we need safer schools, we need to restrain sensationalized media coverage, we need to restore our family values, we need to restore our American values, and we need responsible gun ownership."[37] Amen.

The actor went on to stress the need for measures such as background checks, red flag laws, raising the minimum age to purchase a gun,

---

37 See Kelly Hooper, "Matthew McConaughey at the White House on Gun Reform: 'We Start by Making the Loss of These Lives Matter,'" *Politico*, June 7, 2022, https://www.politico.com/news/2022/06/07/matthew-mcconaughey-gun-reform-00037851.

and establishing a waiting period for the purchase of guns such as AR-15 rifles. He then called on lawmakers to toss partisan politics aside and instead find a middle ground on the issue.

At one point in his speech, tears filled Mr. McConaughey's eyes as he held up the green Converse sneakers (with a heart on the right toe) worn by one of the young victims of the shooting at Uvalde's Robb Elementary School, a ten-year-old girl who would never fulfill her bright promise. He began to lose his composure when he told the audience of reporters about the method of identifying the girl's body. Since the exit wounds created by the assault rifle were so destructive to human flesh, the only way she could be identified was by those signature green sneakers, which she wore to school daily.

So begins this difficult chapter about the onslaught of school shootings and the endless proliferation of violence in America.

There is no doubt that gun violence and school shootings are particularly American phenomena. There have been 2,032 school shootings in the United States since 1970. Alarmingly, 948 of them have taken place since the tragedy of Sandy Hook Elementary School in 2012. Here in America, twelve children die each day from gun violence, and another thirty-two are shot and injured. From the Columbine High School massacre of 1999 to the twenty-one people killed at Robb Elementary in 2022, school shootings have resulted in 169 deaths.[38]

The impact of all this violence on the psyches of children (and adults) is undeniable. For those children who are victims of a school

---

[38] See "17 Facts about Gun Violence and School Shootings," Sandy Hook Promise, https://www. sandyhookpromise.org/blog/gun-violence/16-facts-about-gun-violence-and-school-shootings . See also Associated Press, "From Columbine to Robb, 169 Dead in US Mass School Shootings," *U.S. News & World Report*, May 25, 2022, https://www.usnews.com/news/us/articles/2022-05-24/a-look-at-some-of-the-deadliest-us-school-shootings.

assault, the memories may linger for a lifetime. The most common result is post-traumatic stress disorder. Affected children may be on constant high alert, very jumpy, or very easily angered because of having experienced or witnessed the trauma.

Some children are plagued by feelings of hopelessness, depression, and a self-destructive outlook, while others become emotionally numb. And for more children than we'd like to imagine, this sense of unease, fear, and anxiety is exacerbated by the fact that they have experienced or continue to experience trauma in their own homes. In such circumstances, the nation's children have very good reason to believe that there is truly nowhere they can feel safe.

While many witnesses of school violence will have only temporary symptoms, others will be symptomatic for a long period of time and will even develop chronic psychiatric disorders. But even short-term impairments can cause severe distress and have a profound effect on academic achievement and social and emotional growth.

Elementary school students are particularly vulnerable, perhaps more than adolescents, because they have not yet developed the ability to sort things out in their brains. They have no idea how to make sense of what they've been through.

Even when children aren't directly exposed, they are deeply affected merely by hearing about school shootings. Indeed, one look at the television news or social media coverage of such an event can provoke a sense of fear and anxiety. Disturbing reports about shootings in schools, churches, and stores create a state of hypervigilance, a sense that something terrible is about to happen.

The same goes for all of us—teachers, principals, and parents. Where can we go to feel truly safe? In a 2019 American Psychological Association survey of two thousand people, 62 percent of parents said they lived in fear of their children becoming victims of a mass shooting.[39] Where does that leave us all?

That day in the White House Briefing Room, Mr. McConaughey deftly articulated what so many of us in education have grappled with for years. We must find a long-term solution to gun violence because our children's lives depend on it. Certainly his pleas should resonate with anyone who has a heart, anyone who wants to end this scourge that has violated the sense of safety formerly present in every American school.

In fact, with each new mass shooting event, despite the immense media attention that follows, it feels like the grip of hopelessness gets tighter. Sure, there is a ramping up of rhetoric from politicians in the immediate aftermath of a shooting. Sometimes it even seems to get somewhere, such as the day in June 2022 when President Biden signed a gun safety bill into law. But is that enough? These shootings just keep happening. And they're going to keep happening until our gun-control laws are strengthened even more.

The Roots of Violence

If you're older than, say, thirty, you likely grew up taking for granted that you were safe in your school. Yes, in elementary and secondary schools there might have been an occasional fistfight, but that was the extent of it. No principals expected that their schools would be invaded by assault rifles or that armed guards and bulletproof glass might be needed to protect students.

In those days, we didn't have disgruntled employees, jilted lovers, student pariahs, political extremists, and mentally ill teenagers posting their violent intentions on social media and then carrying them out at a school. It just didn't happen. Those people brought their anger elsewhere.

[39] See Lenny Bernstein et al., "Mass Violence Takes Toll on Americans' Psyches," *Washington Post*, May 27, 2022, https://www.washingtonpost.com/health/2022/05/26/mass-shootings-trauma-effects.

For that reason, I doubt that any of my teachers in the 1960s or 1970s took classes in school safety, nor would anyone think it was a priority. Yes, we conducted fire drills and earthquake and tornado drills. And I am old enough to remember huddling under my desk, cross-legged, with a book on my head because somebody thought that would somehow save us all from the atom bomb.

My elementary and high school teachers were certainly not prepared to hide students behind a barricaded, locked door, mandating complete silence, hoping and praying that their students would all be safe. Likewise, none of my professors in college had a clue about classroom security, nor did any of them receive training in it. In short, we had no need for such a thing.

My initial brush with the threat of school violence occurred in 1991, during my first job as a school principal in Lynchburg, Virginia. Already in place when I arrived was an on-site tutoring program for the poorest students, who lived in a housing project six miles away from the school. But this housing project was plagued by violence and drug abuse. While accompanying some of our staff who volunteered at our on-site after-school tutorial apartment, I observed that the threat of gunfire was present all too often. I will never forget the time when a fourth-grade girl gently but determinedly tugged on my shirt to pull *me* to the floor because she sensed that gunfire was about to erupt outside her apartment window. She was right. That day at the complex, there was some gunfire, though we wound up unharmed—at least physically.

As things got worse at this apartment complex, I received many phone calls from our volunteer tutors' husbands. They all had just one question for me: "Can you guarantee my wife's safety?"

"No," I answered. "I am sorry, but I cannot guarantee that. I wish I could."

Needless to say, our army of volunteers dried up. Our less-than-adequate alternative was to hold the tutoring sessions at school.

And that's when it became crystal clear to me that school should be the kindest, most caring, most supportive place a child can be. Above all, school has to be the *safest* possible place. So even though that housing development was riddled with domestic violence, drug use, and guns, I did everything within my power to make our *school* a secure space.

Indeed, I felt it was our duty to address not only our students' academic needs but also their psychological well-being. Our children needed to be nurtured with a sense of love and belonging. So I worked with teachers, asking them to be sensitive to the way students presented themselves in class. I also asked the teachers to inform me of any student behaviors that would indicate fear or anger or some form of abuse happening at home. In addition, we would talk to troubled students privately and support them in any way we could. Ultimately, the problems in the housing project did not go away, but at least our *school* felt safe. We didn't call it Social Emotional Learning in those days, but that's what it was.[40] Students not only have to be safe at school. They need to *feel* safe as well.

Bottom line: Should school safety be a right? I fervently believe it should be. Look no further than the Declaration of Independence, which guarantees every American the right to life, liberty, and the pursuit of happiness. Yet here we are, struggling to keep schools free from attack. Why is that?

First and foremost, the vast majority of mass shooters have experienced some sort of early childhood trauma and exposure to violence. The nature of this exposure might include physical or sexual abuse, neglect, loss of a parent, domestic violence, and/or severe bullying. All this can lead to serious mental health problems.

[40] See Stephanie M. Jones et al., *Navigating SEL from the Inside Out*, 2nd ed., Harvard Graduate School of Education, July 2021, https://www.wallacefoundation.org/knowledge-center/Documents/navigating-social-and-emotional-learning-from-the-inside-out-2ed.pdf.

Second, most shooters have reached a crisis point during the weeks or months leading up to the shooting. They are often angry and despondent because of a specific grievance.

Third, most mass shooters crave some sort of validation.

Fourth, the shooters all have the means to carry out their plans—that is, they have access to guns.

All this adds up to the fact that mass shooters are very likely to be suffering from mental illness. A teenage shooter might feel like an outsider, or he might feel ostracized or bullied or ignored. Delinquent, antisocial behavior can easily devolve into violent ideation. When mental-health needs go unmet, a sense of isolation, hopelessness, and self-hatred can fester and grow into a hatred for other people, which leads to the desire for revenge.

Lacking coping and self-regulation skills, a shooter will often display either indifference or downright disdain toward his intended target. In some cases, prejudice, hatred, and bigotry are motivating factors. When you add the easy accessibility of guns, you get a perfect storm.

Not least destructive is the impact of social media and violent movies and video games, which can all foster aggression, feeding the psyches of potential bad actors. It's as if instant access to violent content incubates an impulse to strike back. And it becomes ever more seductive to do so when you feel as if you have nothing to lose.

Remember that on social media, loners who are depressed and isolated get instant attention and validation from an anonymous audience *they cannot see.* They lose themselves in the black hole of the Internet, where they can say or do anything they want. On social media, the teenage shooters who were abused, neglected, abandoned, and/or socially ostracized gain instant support and reinforcement.

Disturbingly, social media has even enabled the actions of extremists to be live streamed to viewers. For example, one often overlooked facet of the mass shooting at a Buffalo supermarket in May 2022 is that it was not the work of one person. The shooter brought his thought community with him via live stream. Followers were poised and ready to send out the horrific images of innocent people being slaughtered before Twitch, the social media platform on which he was recording himself, could take it down, which it did in an impressive two minutes. Yet for a few moments, millions of people watched along from home.

In short, social media can be just as powerful a weapon as the high-velocity firearms used in school attacks. I've seen it so often: young people fall into the abyss of gaming or making TikTok videos. They disappear into their online activities for hours or days. Would-be shooters can easily cross the line and begin hanging out in far more dangerous cyberhoods.

Once such a person is detached from the real world and everyday social interaction, common sense is easily suspended. These children lock themselves in their rooms or basements and are alienated from their own families, friends, and classmates. Their former lives are replaced with a completely different reality and set of norms. This social media addiction insinuates itself into the school sooner or later.

For example, the world of TikTok challenges tends to range from the goofy to the merely ill-advised to the truly destructive. I've known of middle schoolers tearing sinks off bathroom walls and stealing their classmates' cell phones so they can memorialize their "accomplishments" on TikTok.

But by all accounts, Shooterland, as opposed to TikTok World, is an extremely dark place where it's standard operating procedure to fantasize about killing children or adults for the mere pleasure of it. And in both cyberworlds, the fantasies are shared by like-minded individuals who are supportive of the intention and celebratory after the act is carried out. That feedback loop is a virtual tornado, gathering up anything and anyone in its path, barreling headlong toward certain destruction.

The so-called truth in these worlds is mostly delusional, distorted by the emotional state of the person posting it. Yet the axes that these social media users have to grind get sharpened by destructive rhetoric that becomes normalized if it's consumed as a steady diet. It all becomes a toxic stew. Social media posts can strongly influence a vulnerable child whose emotions may already be fragile. So that child is swept up in the tornado, at the poster's mercy, to be incited and controlled by what he or she reads.

Safety Protocols and Best Practices

Each time yet another school shooting occurs, it's a gut punch. And it's a horrible reminder that it could happen at *any* school. In fact, if a credible threat of violence forces our school to go into a full or modified lockdown, it creates a ripple of fear among us all. But since we have discussed this, trained for this, and run so many drills for it, there is very little to think about. There is simply reaction. It is like a fire drill but much more intense. The goal is for everyone to reach safety. We all know what to do, including the youngest of our students. To make our response as quick and effective as possible, we follow a basic but very important playbook.

Lock the Doors

First, all doors are to be locked at all times—the exterior doors leading into the building and the classroom and adjoining office doors. The status of these doors is checked continually by our staff, especially by our school resource officer. As I frequently remind everyone, there is no reason on earth to allow the exterior doors of a school to remain unlocked. *Ever.* Ask any teacher who has worked for me about this point. I'm an absolute pain about it. It's a simple concept, but it requires vigilance to enforce. That part of Red Cedar's safety plan has been in place as long as the school has been open.

As for locking classroom doors, that's another story. Before this protocol was put in place, our students had been accustomed to moving freely from one classroom space to another as their schedules dictated— and with the teacher's permission, of course. It was hard for us to hear how important it is to put as many locked doors between ourselves and a potential aggressor as possible. That means we need to lock classroom doors despite the wrinkle it puts in what we regard as part of our school culture. But we're getting over it.

Maintenance and custodial personnel who have propped open doors to the outside and left them that way, even for a short time, have been reassigned, although that hasn't happened in some years. Students, parents, and teachers can rest assured that the physical grounds are checked and secured throughout each day by our staff.

Despite the fact that it is imperative all doors to classrooms and other spaces be lockable, door locks are not likely to be standardized throughout a school district. That means the locks within a given district might not necessarily operate uniformly and might not be maintained at a consistently high level. Our school was built in 2009, so the locks on our classroom doors all work pretty much the same way and are kept in good working order.

Some teachers in schools throughout the country who have been through an active shooter event have lamented the need to lock classroom doors from the *outside*, as having to exit the classroom to do so once a lockdown is called potentially puts them in the path of the shooter. Our teachers avoid this by locking their classroom doors from the outside first thing in the morning and keeping them in the locked position all day. It is important for them to be certain the doors are locked *before* anything happens rather than have to struggle in the heat of the moment.

Here's a sad fact. Twice in the last two years, when we had planned to have a lockdown drill, we had to reschedule them. One time it was because a shooting had occurred at a school somewhere in the country the day before. The other one was because a shooting had happened that very day. Clearly our collective nerves would not be able to sustain the rigors of a drill either of those days.

Additional Precautions

In the event of a security threat, our safety protocols at Red Cedar, like those of the rest of our school district, include the following.

- Now always a part of our procedures, visitors press a button outside the front doors to state their business via intercom. We view them via a camera built into the communication system. We meet them outside the school to handle all issues that do not require their entering the building. It was initially a COVID protocol, but it has safety implications as well. For example, sometimes a parent is agitated. If the situation requires my intervention or that of the school resource officer, we'd much rather have what we hope will be a calming conversation outside of the school instead of inside. (Sometimes an audience enhances an obstreperous parent's desire to raise the drama level. We don't need that.)

- Surveillance cameras are strategically placed both inside and outside the school (although not in the bathrooms or the classrooms), and we continually check the angle of those cameras for any areas that may be obscured. Of course, we have the ability to review footage and preserve screenshots from the cameras.

- We also have a full complement of working two-way radios. The radios used by our first responders and law enforcement professionals are viable in our buildings, too, so we can all communicate effectively.

- Anyone who parks in our parking lot or anywhere on the property and appears as if they are planning to remain there or does not appear to have any business at the school is observed and confronted. We are pleasant but firm. No, you can't play soccer here while school is in session. No, this isn't the place to file your expense report. No, you can't watch the students while you're on a lunch break. May I give you directions to the nearest park?

Obviously, we work closely with all law enforcement agencies and first-responder organizations that serve the county. Together, we have developed contingency plans for a wide variety of emergencies. Officers and other professionals test these plans in our schools before training the school district's staff.

Despite all the hypervigilance, I must say that our school remains a pleasant place to be. It does not feel like a locked-down prison. By now, all students, staff, and parents understand the safety measures that have been put into place. The magic is still the magic, and the joy is still the joy. Students and staff are happy to be there.

Step-by-Step Lockdown Procedure

Once emergency protocols are established, we conduct regular lockdown drills. The following is the district's standard procedure.

- Should a threat appear, an announcement is made over both the PA system and the two-way radios that a lockdown is in place. If it is a drill, we state that clearly in the announcement. The announcement is made twice. We train all staff to be prepared to call a lockdown and announce it themselves: we don't want to waste valuable time by having the staff member who is privy to the danger try to find an administrator to make the call.

- Shortly after the lockdown is called, I use the Remind app on my phone to contact those staff members who were able to grab their phones before fleeing or sheltering.

- A designated staff member calls 911 and, if time permits, the school district office as well.

- If possible, anyone who can scans the hallway closest to them for students who were caught in the hallway when the lockdown was called. Those adults scoop up those students and adopt them as their own.

- If an emergency occurs during one of the lunch periods, the students are taken to the nearest safe area. The teachers and staff on lunch duty remain with the students until the situation is secure.
- Students on the playground have all practiced with our school resource officer how to run and where to go to escape.
- Unless otherwise directed, students who are in classrooms during lunch are kept there until the all clear is announced.
- Law enforcement professionals clear the rooms, one by one, once the event or the drill is concluded.
- Teachers choose if they and those in their care will shelter or will run from the building. That is situational and based primarily on information at hand.
- Afterward, every teacher documents the activity that occurred during the emergency and offers suggestions as to how things could have been better managed.
- Our community information people get the word out via our Bright Arrow alert system that an event is taking place, stating specifically what the event is and providing follow-ups as appropriate.

Staff Responsibilities

Teachers and administrators are protectors in an emergency, though they also have the expectation of being protected. While they may be scared beyond belief, they need to be strong and calm and inspire confidence in their students. We are not professional first responders. We are zero-time responders. We are at once experiencing the trauma and providing relief to our students.

Following are some of the responsibilities we carry out and rules we abide by in the event of a threat.

- Assist students with special needs and/or disabilities.

- Doors and windows should already be closed and locked. Pull the shades down.
- Do not leave the room in which you are sheltering or allow anyone else to leave for any reason.
- Stay away from the door and windows.
- Shut off the lights.
- Disregard all bells and alarms.
- Direct students to the floor if gunshots or explosions are heard.
- Be prepared to remain in lockdown for an extended period of time.
- If directed to evacuate, instruct students to leave their personal belongings behind.
- *Be quiet.*
- Wait for further instruction from an administrator or a police officer via phone or in person.

Stockpile Jacobs Kits

Because individuals injured in a mass casualty event might be sheltered in a room for an extended period of time without the assistance of first responders, lifesaving treatment may not be available. After the tragedy at Sandy Hook Elementary School in 2012, a Connecticut trauma surgeon, Dr. Lenworth Jacobs Jr., convened a panel to evaluate on-site responses to such emergencies. The team's goal was to enable anyone to use a tourniquet to stop an injury victim from bleeding to death.

The result of that work is the Jacobs Kit.[41]

Our school received the kits we have through the generosity of a retired FBI agent, the grandfather of a girl who was then a student at Red Cedar. Schools throughout our district have received kits in a variety

---

[41] For more information and to order kits, see the website of the nonprofit organization Stop the Bleed: https://www.stopthebleed.org.

of ways. And we were trained by EMTs in the use of the kits—just as we were trained in the use of our automated external defibrillators—but we hope we never have to use that training.

Fighting Back

No matter how thorough our preparations may be, we can't prepare for everything. So district policy in active shooter situations requires that principals and teachers make one key decision: Is it better to shelter behind as many locked doors as possible, without leaving the room one is in at the time? Or is it better to take students away from the building?

In making that decision, staff members must take into account the age of the students in their classrooms and their physical abilities. Clearly, deciding to flee with a group of seventh graders is a vastly different proposition than attempting that act with a bunch of kindergartners. Mind you, this is an individual decision. That is, if a teacher determines for a whole host of reasons that evacuating the building is the best route, that's what he will do. If it seems best to shelter in place, that will happen instead. During one drill, three teachers decided independently to evacuate the building. They all knew where they were headed and arrived there quickly. Our school resource officer and our recess monitors continue to practice these drills.

If the choice is to stay in the school, part of that decision might include fighting back. It always includes covering the small window built into the door so no one can see into the classroom (teachers have a scroll-down shade that can be easily pulled over the window; at all other times that window is to remain uncovered for other safety reasons). The lights are turned off according to protocol, and everyone remains silent. The idea is to convince the intruder that this classroom is empty: nothing to see here; don't bother with this room.

One of the teachers at our school ushers all his students into a small room within his classroom. He then locks that outer door and stands next to it in the dark with a baseball bat in his hand, poised to use it as if he's standing at home plate. Other teachers use golf clubs or other sports equipment as their weapons of choice.

Then there are barricades and other tricks teachers employ to keep the bad guy out. For example, there is a way you can wedge a student chair under a door handle that makes it virtually impossible to enter the classroom, even with a key. At the end of each drill, police officers and administrators unlock the doors and attempt to gain access to classrooms that have been barricaded this way from the inside. Much to our relief, they are unable to every time. Probably the only really positive moments as we go from door to door, beyond the fact that we are all "free" again, involve seeing the looks on the teachers' and students' faces when a police officer who's built like a linebacker cannot get through the teacher's carefully constructed barriers.

Stay Calm

All preparations, precautions, and procedures must be executed efficiently and without emotion, or at least without the expression of it. Even the tone of the voice on the PA system must be authoritative, calm, and clear. We need the speaker to sound serious but not scare or panic the children, because we need them to be attentive and cooperatively follow all instructions.

Sadly, I'm not saying that we as teachers and administrators can provide our students with a total safety *guarantee*. I wish we could. But we are going to do everything we can to protect them and keep them safe. We also want them to *feel* safe, no matter what. Still, on stressful occasions such as a lockdown, even when all the protocols are followed, I still have questions. Our administrative team and school resource officer always debrief to determine whether we could have done a better job and whether we have any issues with the building that need addressing.

Not least, as the principal, I also must assess the management skills of our substitute teachers on duty that day. Who among them might be easily rattled? How well were they trained to manage a crisis in the class-room? Are there any substitutes here today who are weak links?

In the late 1990s, when I was the principal at the Saltonstall School, I had an experience that certainly put me to the test. One unseasonably warm day in February, I was surprised to receive a call from the acting superintendent of schools, who told me he had just gotten word that an armed bank robber was leading law enforcement on a high-speed chase. Shots had already been fired, and the perpetrator was headed toward Salem.

Because our school was located on the town's main road, I felt as if every one of the eighty third graders, then outside during recess, was a potential target. That is, if this perpetrator were cornered, it might be easy in such a desperate situation for him to snatch up a child to hold as a hostage. So as calmly as I could, I radioed the two supervising assistants outside to direct all the children back inside the school—*immediately*—giving no reason for the action. "Just start lining them up," I said. "Don't let anyone lag, and I will get there to assist as soon as possible."

Back in those days, we were flying by the seat of our pants: there were no protocols for shooter drills or school lockdowns. I just followed my instincts, which obviously included checking every door in the school to make sure it was locked.

When I got outside, many of the students were confused and unhappy about the abrupt change in plans. "What's going on?" they implored. "Why are we leaving?"

The teachers and I made it clear that we were not entertaining any questions.

"Why not?" they asked. "We *always* ask questions!" This was what we had taught them to do in the classroom.

But this was not a class. "Nope," I said. "No questions today. Just do it because I said so. Sometimes you have to follow instructions without asking why. This is one of those times."

As I thought about it later, I took some pride in the persistence of our nine-year-olds. Intellectual curiosity is something to be cultivated. And student questions are a critical first step in solving problems and improving high-level thinking skills. But in an emergency situation, with a shooter near at hand, those questions must be shelved for the greater good.

Within minutes, the students and staff were safe inside, unaware of the threat or the media presence growing in our little town. Throughout the afternoon, my instinct was a maternal one—to protect our children and keep them from worry and danger.

The incident took a dangerous turn when a young dad with his four-year-old twins was held hostage in his own home by the robber. Coincidentally, the dad was the brother of one of our staff members. But fortunately, neither he nor his sons were injured, and the perpetrator was apprehended.

The biggest lesson of the day: if this could happen once, it could happen again, and we needed guidelines for handling subsequent incidents safely and quickly.

The following day, I spoke to each class individually about what to do when a caring adult you know looks at you and gives you an order. "It won't happen very often," I said, "but when it does, just do what you're told."

I've also used this example or a pared-down version of it when talking to parents who seem to value the exercise of their child's free will over the development of other attributes, especially when they are defending their child's recalcitrant actions. I ask if, as a family, they have a safety plan for situations that demand their child listen without objection. For instance, a code that says, *Come to me this second!* without actually saying that. Most are initially surprised that I or anyone else thinks that this is something that requires attention. After giving it some thought, though, they generally make such a plan and practice it with their child.

Ever since that day, I have made this simple point to students: under emergency circumstances, just listen and comply.

Look for Warning Signs

After all these years have passed, and after hundreds of school shootings have taken place, you would think school staff members might get used to it. Never. Each time we learn about a school shooting, it feels like the movie *Groundhog Day*—a loop we can't get out of. And I feel just slightly less safe than I did before.

The day after any school shooting occurs, no matter how far away, I meet with our student services team, which includes the school resource officer, our guidance counselor, our social worker, the assistant principal, our behavior management specialist, and the school nurse. We review the known facts of the incident and compare how our protocols would hold up against a similar attack, looking for anything we need to change.

In November 2021, we discussed the case of Ethan Crumbley, the fifteen-year-old student at Oxford High School in Oxford Township, Michigan, who fatally shot four students and wounded seven other people, including a teacher. On the day of the attack, school personnel had good reason to believe the boy was dangerous. They told his parents to seek counseling for him within forty-eight hours or they would call child protective services. In the meantime, they recommended that the boy be removed from class and taken home, but the parents refused. Backing down, the school officials simply allowed the teenager to remain on campus. Two hours later, the shooting started.

Did that have to happen? We'll never know.

Our school discussion centered on one major question: How would we have handled the fact that the parents did not want to take their son home? We agreed that given the warning signs, our school resource officer would have removed the boy—and his backpack—from the school. The student would either have been taken home and released to his parents or referred to law enforcement. In any case, he would have been kept away from the school while undergoing observation and counseling.

But even prior to that, our counselor and social worker would have looked for signs of depression, anxiety, and aggression. When there are warning signs of such emotional turbulence, we take them very seriously. For example, if a child is expressing thoughts of violence against himself or others, we're right on it. Even if a child is not forthcoming, staff members notice changes in behavior. Other students sometimes notice them as well.

Of course, we understand that some students *live* in trauma as a result of difficult home circumstances. Physical violence, marital strife, and drug and alcohol use can all profoundly affect a child's state of mind. A student arriving at school in the morning may already be feeling a high level of anxiety. But I can tell you that when something is not right, one or more of us already feels it. Who is the person on staff who has the best relationship with this child? That's the person who will talk with the student if something seems off. Information that comes out of that conversation usually helps so we can intervene and serve that student, giving him the emotional support he needs.

In the case of the Michigan school shooter, we would certainly not have been swayed by the parents' nonchalant attitude toward their son's behavior. Nor would we have allowed the child to linger at the school.

Legislation

As a longtime school principal, I am often frustrated by the lawmakers who extend their sympathies to bereaved parents while underperforming when it comes to tightening up gun laws and exploring the consistent enforcement of existing laws—or anything that might move the nation closer to solving this daunting and dangerous problem. At times, fierce defenders of the Second Amendment are absurd in their arguments.

To underscore my point, I give you this rare gem: "In rural Colorado, an AR-15 is the weapon of choice for killing raccoons before they get to our chickens," noted Representative Ken Buck (R-CO) as he advocated maintaining the status quo on the availability of such rifles. How a seemingly intelligent, articulate legislator could advance such an argument—that his constituents' chickens are more important than the safety of the nation's children—is beyond my comprehension. It's obviously a ridiculous premise, a reach to defend an indefensible stance on assault weapons, designed for a particularly receptive audience of like-minded crazy-powerful gun-o-philes.

In a country where there are more firearms than people, priorities need to be rearranged. If the law enforcement personnel on the scene at Robb Elementary School in Uvalde, Texas, were, shall we say, hesitant to confront a gunman with a high-powered firearm when they had him significantly outnumbered (376 to 1), how can parents feel that their children have a chance when they're under attack?

Let's review: those officers in Uvalde were dressed in body armor and were holding shields, while the children had nothing at all to protect them. What does that tell us about the state of policing as it relates to maintaining public safety? This is all very discouraging indeed. A total mess from start to finish. This cannot happen again.

Were those officers afraid to storm the hallways and take out the gunman because of the weapon he carried? If that is the case, no amount of training and protocol will be of any use. Did the officers abandon those children because weapons of war frighten them—the very people whose sworn duty is to serve and protect citizens?

Teachers should teach. Yes, they need to be concerned about their students' safety. But no teacher should have to be prepared to shield students from bullets in the classroom. Maybe we should not have to choose between a gun enthusiast's right to buy a weapon of war or a child's right to live to a ripe old age. But if we *must* choose between the two, isn't the decision obvious?

PART FOUR

Maintaining School Climate and Culture

CHAPTER 9

It's What We Do

Going the Extra Mile

YEARS AGO, WHEN I WAS A MUSIC TEACHER, I WAS LIKE A traveling troubadour, assigned to three schools at the same time. I enjoyed the variety that going from school to school afforded, but unfortunately, when you don't have the consistency of daily contact with a group of students, it's difficult to get to know them.

I am observant though. And in some ways, I was the one getting an education, experiencing the contrasting cultures of three different environments, which was incredibly eye-opening.

I'll never forget the time I was in the teachers' workroom at one of the schools where I taught. The ten of us in the room suddenly heard the cry of a young child coming from the hallway. It wasn't a terrible shriek, but the child who made the sound was clearly in distress. Nearly everyone looked up. But no one immediately moved toward the sound.

After a few seconds, the teacher closest to the door looked into the hallway, returned to the room, and, astoundingly, announced, "Not mine." This was her way of saying that she was unconcerned and not interested in the pain of the child. In fact, she then continued copying documents and microwaving her lunch. Two other teachers and I made eye contact and immediately went out into the hallway to find a kindergarten girl named Jill holding her right knee. She had just suffered a scrape from a fall. Her cry came from the shock of seeing her own blood.

We escorted Jill to the nurse's office, talking to her quietly, calming her along the way. This situation remains in my memory to this day as a prime example of what I would call poor school culture. Why? Because the teacher who refused to help Jill was willfully ignoring a child's immediate needs. Her carelessness and lack of responsibility were appalling. Worse yet, she was clearly not alone on the staff in her approach.

Had I been the principal in charge, I would never have tolerated this kind of callous behavior. It goes against everything I know about a good school culture—a highly supportive environment that is responsive first and foremost to the needs of students but also to the needs of the staff and parents. The guiding beliefs and values at such a school create a safe and healthful physical and emotional environment no matter what the circumstances. A solid, positive school culture is the soul of the school.

Jill should have been at recess, watched over by other staff members, instead of walking alone down that hallway. It was early in the school year, and generally kindergartners were not left to navigate the hallways of the school alone. She had somehow fallen through the cracks and needed help. Yet nobody in that workroom sprang up upon hearing her. When trained teachers don't respond to a child literally crying out for help, there's a problem. And to have a teacher say, "Not mine," as in, "I see no reason to interrupt what I am doing because she is not my responsibility," speaks volumes. Not least disturbing, one of the staff members in our workroom actually *was* the girl's teacher. She should have been front and center as a "first responder" in this incident. But she wasn't. Honestly, she seemed more interested in her ham-and-cheese sandwich than anything else.

This wasn't the first or last time I experienced a school culture like this, far from it. After that incident, I made a pact with myself that if I ever led a school, I would not tolerate anything remotely similar. More importantly, I would help lead a culture that made that kind of behavior unheard of; no one would even think that way. Any school that claims to have a positive culture could not possibly abide such a scene. If you hear a child crying, you go toward that sound. It's what you do because you care—or you should.

This story leads me to my main point: positive culture is critical to every school's success. For me, it's what makes a school special—or not. It's the organization's core beliefs as they are put into practice. In a positive culture, there is a sense of camaraderie that will permeate everything and everyone associated with the school. Such a culture feels energetic and upbeat. You can see that teachers and students work well together, striving to achieve common goals.

In my experience, an increasing number of savvy administrators have come to understand the value of fostering a positive school culture. And their devotion to it is often measured by school districts and state departments of education.

One assessment instrument that measures school culture is offered by a company called Upbeat, an educational service that provides "targeted data collection and consulting to improve school culture and increase teacher retention."[42] A survey administered to teachers measures twenty-three dimensions of school culture by assessing that school's climate.[43] In any organization, you want both of those to be solid. The following are aspects of their experience that teachers were asked about.

---

[42] For more information, check out Upbeat at https://www.teachupbeat.com.

[43] Climate and culture, technically speaking, are two different things. According to the National School Climate Center, climate is the "quality and character of school life." Culture, on the other hand, is more deeply ingrained and encompasses "a school's norms, unwritten rules, traditions, and expectations." See Elisabeth Kane et al., "School Climate & Culture," University of Nebraska-Lincoln, February 2016, https://k12engagement.unl.edu/strategy-briefs/School%20 Climate%20&%20Culture%202-6-16%20.pdf.

- Parent-teacher communication: Is it frequent? Are staff members accessible? Are there several ways to keep in contact? Are several languages available?
- Professional development: Are appropriate ongoing learning opportunities provided for staff members? Is there a spirit of continual learning among adults?
- Autonomy: Do teachers feel like they have a voice in what is taught, how it is taught, and at the pace it is taught? Do teachers feel "lockstepped"?
- Principal-teacher trust: Do teachers feel as though administrators in the building have their backs when situations, especially with parents, get dicey?
- Instructional leadership: Do the administrators inspire confidence among the staff and school community? Do they know what is best academically, socially, physically, and emotionally for all students? Are they willing to act on that knowledge? Are they willing to take suggestions from staff?
- School safety and order: Do the administrators care deeply about student and staff welfare? Do they follow the directives from the school district that promote the safety and security of everyone for whom they are responsible?
- Appreciation: Are teachers noticed and acknowledged for their efforts? Are they congratulated for student growth? Is there a general tenor of gratitude among administrators for the work that staff members do every day?
- Collaboration: Is working cooperatively valued in the school? Does cooperation occur naturally or does it need to be enforced by administrators?
- Work-life balance: What is considered the appropriate amount of time to dedicate to teaching? How do those requirements compare

with the demands of life outside of school? Are the expectations reasonable?

- Resources and facilities: What is the condition of the building? How old is it? How old does it feel?
- Self-efficacy: How do all stakeholders feel about their ability to effect change? How do they feel about their ability to succeed? If there are bumps in this road, who helps smooth the way?
- Evaluation: Is the teacher observation and evaluation process administered fairly, with the ideals of growth and increasing capacity in mind? What happens when a teacher falls short of expectations? Is there an appropriately employed plan in place to "coach up" staff members who need it?
- Teacher voice and leadership: Do teachers have a say in the policy direction the school takes? Are teachers consulted about finding and addressing needs within and across grade levels?
- Recruitment, hiring, and onboarding: Do staff members have a role in recruiting their own colleagues? Do they review résumés, write interview questions, interview the candidates, and acclimate new hires to the school's procedures?
- Compensation and career path: Is the pay scale commensurate with that of nearby districts? Is the salary schedule fairly administered? Are there opportunities for advancement and movement into other departments?
- Belonging and well-being: Do people like working at the school? Do they feel as though they can contribute positively to the mission of the school?
- Diversity: Is there a range of ethnic and social backgrounds represented in the school?
- Equity: Are policies and procedures designed and carried out so that all parties are treated with fairness and impartiality? When

there are questions about equity, can administrators look critically at the situation and make changes if necessary?

- Inclusion: Does the school provide equal access to opportunities for everyone in the school community? Does the school build bridges that enable students (especially special-needs and second-language students) to make academic progress?
- Cultural competence: Is the school sensitive to members of a variety of cultures? Do staff members recognize differences and celebrate what is best about every culture?
- Care and commitment: Do staff members treat students, parents, and one another with kindness and compassion? Do they genuinely care for one another?
- Student engagement: Are students interested in and in charge of their learning? Do teachers design their lessons to capture their students' attention and increase their participation?
- Satisfaction and purpose: Do staff members feel as if they are making a difference? Do they take pride in their accomplishments? Do the teachers and assistants believe their work is critically important and the most valuable use of their time?

Creating a Positive School Climate

The following are just a few examples of the ways in which we create a positive school climate at Red Cedar Elementary.

Committed Parent-Teacher Communication

It is ever so easy to give up on parent-teacher communication. The principal says, "Did you meet with Mrs. Harrison?" The teacher says, "I really tried, but she wouldn't return my phone calls. Then after we finally connected and made an appointment, she stood me up. I just stopped trying." Big mistake, young teacher. Big mistake. You stay in there, and you keep pitching. "Do you need help? I'll go with you for a surprise visit."

Ongoing Professional Development

At Red Cedar Elementary, teacher training takes place at the weekly meetings of our professional learning communities.[44] Our academic coaches and grade-level leaders (teachers who want more responsibility and are willing to collaborate with, coach, and teach the folks on their team) guide the practice of our teachers. Important work takes place in these meetings, and we are better for it. The dialogue focuses on student learning, emphasizes collaboration, and fosters inquiry and reflection. Many an epiphany has occurred during and after these rich discussions.

Respect for Teacher Autonomy

My philosophy on this subject is probably best summarized by a fourth-grade teacher who had been at our school for three years. She said, "Dr. Corley, I know that if I have an idea I think will benefit my students, and if I'm willing to plan it and devise a way to assess its effectiveness, you will likely let me try it, because you know that I'll try really hard to make it work. You realize that I'll probably work harder on my own idea than I will on an idea suggested in a teachers' guide." And she was right. There is a lot to be gained for the teacher *and* the students if the teacher is encouraged to follow her heart while doing what's best for her students.

---

44 The scholar Shirley M. Hord defines "professional learning community" as a method of "extending classroom practice into the community, ... bringing community personnel into the school to enhance the curriculum and learning tasks for students, ... [and] having students, teachers, and administrators reciprocally engaged in learning." See Shirley M. Hord, "Professional Learning Communities: Communities of Continuous Inquiry and Improvement," Office of Educational Research and Improvement, US Department of Education, 1997, https://sedl.org/pubs/change34/plc-cha34.pdf.

I'm proud to say that the school climate and culture scores at Red Cedar Elementary are consistently high. This is also reflected in our success in many other aspects of student achievement. In 2022, the South Carolina School Report Cards, issued by the state's department of education, showed academic as well as climate and culture score declines for many schools across the state compared to 2019, when the scores had last been recorded. Ours was *not* one of those schools. By contrast, 20 percent of the state's schools were rated as excellent—meaning that a school "substantially exceeds the criteria to ensure all students meet the Profile of the SC Graduate." Ours *was* among those schools. In addition to academic ratings, the report card includes a climate rating. Had we not achieved an excellent climate rating, we would not have scored an overall excellent rating.[45]

In 2014, we decided to apply for the Palmetto's Finest award, the highest educational honor in the state, bestowed by the South Carolina Association of School Administrators. The judging is a rigorous process that evaluates student achievement, school culture, and a school's professional learning community. There is a detailed application to complete, and then, if the school becomes a finalist, two on-site visits.

Two elementary schools per year are chosen for the award. Rarely does a Title I school—one that serves a large percentage of students at or near the poverty level—win this award. But we did. We had perfect scores for the components that helped the Palmetto's Finest committee tease out what kind of culture we had created in our school. When that announcement was made, in front of all our students and staff, it was a scene of utter joy. All our work had been validated; beyond our impressive growth in student achievement, Red Cedar was and is a place where families and staff want to be.

---

45 Our report card can be accessed at "Red Cedar Elementary School," SC School Report Card, https://screportcards.com/overview/?q=eToyMDIyJnQ9RSZzaWQ9MDcwMTAzNA.

Our teacher-retention percentages are high as well because we nurture and support our staff. When there is a "disturbance in the Force"—a disruption in any aspect of school culture—we take a step back to analyze what is not working. For example, we do not have many general staff meetings: ours is not a "we have a weekly meeting whether we need it or not" kind of place. But every so often, a brief attitude changer in the form of a "stand-up" (very short) meeting for those who are available can provide the antidote to something that just doesn't feel right.

In addition to the Upbeat data report, schools in our district rely on surveys administered by the state and the school district that evaluate student engagement and students' views of their own abilities and achievements. All these help us assess our school culture. But beyond formal testing, I can tell you that positive school culture is something you can intuitively sense. It's a vibe that sets the tone for everything that happens in the school. For most people I know in education, discussions about school culture begin and end with, "You can just feel it when you walk around the school."

In fact, after giving a family a tour of the school, if one of the adults says, "I wish *I* could go to school here!" we consider it among the highest compliments we can receive. It's easy for them to see that our teachers engage with students and connect with them in a personalized way. Parents also react to the atmosphere of sheer fun in our classrooms. They see a teacher showing enthusiasm as she demonstrates the difference between liquids and solids. They pick up on the students' equally enthusiastic response. They glance at one another. They smile. We move on. "Is that the list of all the clubs you have for your students after school? Amazing."

We make our way through the hallways as students change classes. A second grader stops his line to give our small party the opportunity to cross in front of him. He might even bow slightly with his hand out, smiling, to make sure we get the hint that this is being done for us. This is not lost on the visitors.

We nurture our values and expected behaviors, even displaying them in common areas. Posters are mounted on the walls around the school with messages such as "How do Foxes behave in the hallway?" with accompanying agreed-on rules that can be referenced anytime the situation calls for it. Safety is important. Order is important. After those are established, all that's left to do is learn and have fun.

Note that I've focused much more on culture than on climate. Climate is a somewhat fleeting sort of thing. It's about the way we feel, which can ebb and flow to a certain extent even in the healthiest of schools. Culture is far more pervasive. It's who we are and what we prize, and it's what we will go to the mat to protect and nurture.

Whatever It Takes

At Red Cedar Elementary, my personal motto and our school mantra is "Whatever it takes." When we opened the school in 2009, I saw before me a blank canvas of possibility, a shiny brand-new school that could embody the best that a bunch of talented, dedicated professionals could dream up.

A good example of "Whatever it takes" is our support of a struggling kindergartner named Lowell. Bright and inquisitive, Lowell is a child with autism who was not accustomed to boundaries. It was pretty much Lowell's way or the highway as far as he was concerned. Building bridges between the way Lowell thought things ought to go and the way we thought they ought to go took time and patience. For one thing, he has sensory-sensitivity issues and had not yet developed appropriate mechanisms to cope with them. He was just beginning to learn how to navigate the world as a person with unique needs.

So we formed a Team Lowell, a group of seven and sometimes eight professionals who examined every aspect of his day at school, and often beyond, to identify the challenges he faced. The team—which included a school district psychologist, a classroom teacher, a behavior management specialist, a literacy support professional, a classroom assistant, a district autism specialist, and an administrator (and sometimes a counselor, social worker, or speech pathologist)—devised a plan to determine how those challenges could be overcome.

The membership of such teams can vary depending on the student. For example, our PE teacher has a great way with the students who tend to show little ability to self-regulate and adapt to new surroundings and circumstances. She is frequently a member of those special teams because she cares so deeply and is so incredibly talented at it. There have been others over the years, but Mrs. Black stands out.

The members of Team Lowell kept in close contact with one another, sharing what worked and what didn't and encouraging Lowell with some attaboys when he reached new milestones. His success was their success. In a broader sense, their success is also the school community's success. We also learn a lot from our Lowells and from all our students, fueling our growth and therefore our ability to meet other students' needs.

Still, you might argue that no school can afford to devote as much attention as we did to all the Lowells it might have at any given time. Isn't that too many people and too much time? No. "Whatever it takes" is the answer, regardless of the question, because a positive school culture is based on sensitivity to the needs of each child and his or her family. We can always widen our circle, within and outside our school staff, to address the needs of other Lowells.

A school has to make a commitment to be there for their students and families. The Lowells of the world need us in order to reach their potential. Our goal is to help them believe they can do just that. We need to take the journey with them and celebrate them when they've reached their goals.

So our mantra, "Whatever it takes," is not a vague, tired catchphrase. Instead, it describes our uncompromising dedication to engaging all our students in learning so that they can achieve at the highest level possible, regardless of their economic background (most of our students are economically disadvantaged), their parents' level of involvement, the language they speak, and any hurdles they need to surmount in order to live their best academic lives.

"Whatever it takes"—you might think that's a nice slogan but certainly not a commitment shared by all adults in the building. There must be some teachers, assistants, and support staff who don't buy into the party line. Certainly there are: but over time, we usually get them to change their minds. They either step up or move on. As they learn, the "Red Cedar Way" requires a tremendous investment of energy, a daily commitment to creating magic in the classroom. To me, our school culture is the culmination of everything I've learned during a lifetime in education. We have been able to put it in place and nurture it with the help and support of like-minded district personnel, parents, colleagues, the community, and the students themselves.

Traditions

Routines. Procedures. Innovative ideas. Going the extra mile. Customs. All these speak to school culture. The annual kickball game between the fifth graders and the teaching staff at Red Cedar is an essential part of that. The teachers are undefeated. We have T-shirts that say so. But in the year that COVID-19 snatched the tradition away from us, a couple of the fifth graders—who had been waiting at least two years to have their shot at knocking us off our perch—had their own shirts printed. Those were emblazoned with WE WON THE KICKBALL GAME. THE TEACHERS FORFEITED.

Red Cedar Stew, like Saltonstall Stew, is another tradition. Born for different reasons in two different schools, they live on for the same reason: it's what we do.

Here's a more solemn tradition: the entire population of Red Cedar, adult and child, sings the national anthem around the flagpole on September 14 to celebrate the writing of "The Star-Spangled Banner" in 1814. In addition, each year, on or near Veterans Day, we pay our respects to all who have served in our nation's armed forces.

As part of the remembrance, the America's White Table ceremony is performed with incredible reverence by fifth graders. It honors captured soldiers and their families who waited for their return, and involves pushing an empty chair to the table, laying a black napkin alongside a place setting, and turning a glass over, thereby symbolizing the meal that would not be eaten with their absence. It gets me every time. It's what we do.

One year, there was a natural disaster in a Central American country. We sent bottled water to some great folks who found a way to get it where it needed to go. We wrote messages on the labels to bolster spirits. A year later, upon hearing his teacher mention that there were new flooding problems after a hurricane in another country, one boy said, "There's just one thing to do." He sat at his table, took out some paper, and fished around in his pencil caddy. He noticed a few other students looking at him quizzically. "What?" he said. "It's time to collect water and write nice notes!" Even this little guy knew: it's what we do. We leave things better than the way we found them.

Apple Pie and Red Velvet Cake

Kelly Wersler works hard at Red Cedar to help make us the school family we are. But her job title, academic coach, is not an adequate description of her many functions. As a coach, she helps teachers become the best educators they can be through training, modeling, and encouragement. She also provides one-on-one guidance to students during difficult moments.

For example, during the time COVID-19 forced schools to operate online, Kelly visited the Mayweather household, which consisted of a mom and her three children, the mom's sister's two children, their mother, and their grandmother. The teachers of the five youngsters had been unable to reach the parents either by phone or by email. Assignments were falling through the cracks. So Kelly went to the house to find out the facts, assess needs, and persuade the adults to participate more actively in the children's education. For the children to be successful, it would require all key players to participate.

Kelly was understandably more than a bit surprised when the door was opened by an overwhelmed-looking elderly woman holding a folded strip of leather in her hand. She was yelling over her shoulder, "I told you to learn your ABCs! Get over here!" In a gesture of deference, Kelly stepped back from the front door.

At that moment, having encountered a complicated situation, she was forced to decide between "tattling" on the children for falling behind in their work or getting the adults to realize the importance of getting involved. Ultimately, she decided that the visit wasn't about going through a checklist of what the teachers wanted. It was about forming a plan to do better—helping the children *want* to do better.

Great-Grandma said, "I don't play. I'm old. I've already done this. I raised my kids; now I'm raisin' some more." Kelly assured her that all was well from the school's point of view and said that she just wanted to talk a bit. You see, she got the sense that although the teachers were becoming frustrated with the lack of attention the family was giving to all things school-related, the adults in the household were probably overwhelmed and doing the best they could do—with no one honoring their contribution.

Kelly bent down to face the children eye to eye. "I think you know why I'm here." They nodded in agreement, savvy enough to understand that this visit was indeed about their not doing their work. But Kelly wasn't going to say that out loud. The children's eyes dropped toward the floor.

That sealed the deal for Kelly. In a purposeful tone, she said, "I'm here to find out if you need some new books." When their eyes suddenly lifted again, she added, "So that you can become fantastic readers."

Around this time, Kelly realized she had caught Great-Grandma's attention. She stood back up. "I'm also here to get Great-Grandma some help."

Kelly chatted amiably with the woman, trying to figure out what support systems she needed. But she knew that wasn't enough. She knew the family needed more, and it had to be tangible.

On the drive back to school, Kelly wondered about the last time someone had done something nice for that family. How long ago had it been?

After hearing about the meeting, I stared at Kelly in disbelief. "You said what? They did what? She had what in her hand?" Kelly assured me that all was well because she now knew how we could make a difference with this family.

Clearly, the matriarch of the Mayweather family was overwhelmed and underequipped to deal with a house full of children. And like so many other hardworking caretakers, she was faced with many obstacles, including poverty, medical problems, emotional trauma brought on by the sudden deaths of more than one family member, and the transience of her great-grandchildren's stay with her. It wasn't certain whether they would remain with her or move in with other relatives. The ambiguity itself was unsettling. It was as if the family was sinking, with one metaphorical foot stuck in a hole. Kelly wanted to fill that hole, and I wanted to help her do it.

That night, I called Kelly to report that the hard-to-reach Mayweather mom had finally called, perplexed that we had "sent a social worker" after her. She mistakenly believed we had reported her to the South Carolina Department of Social Services. During the call, I could hear Great-Grandma yelling at the children about doing their homework. Mrs. Mayweather apologetically noted that her mother could yell sometimes, and everyone just understood that.

In a follow-up call to the grand-mom, Kelly didn't directly confront the great-grandmother's way of wrangling her great-grandchildren. Instead, she opted for a more indirect—and effective—approach. She told the mom that within a few weeks she would bring the most senior Mayweather a couple of desserts. She had found out that her sweets of choice were red velvet cake and apple pie. Kelly handled the first, and I took care of the second, a lattice-topped number with big sugar crystals dotting the crust, made from a recipe that won an award in our neighborhood baking contest some years ago.

When Kelly and I arrived at the Mayweather place a week or so later, we had the apple pie and a carefully chosen selection of books in hand. They were "leveled books," chosen by experienced professionals who know what students want to read—teachers, literacy interventionists, and academic coaches—to appropriately challenge each of the children. Kelly brought around four books per child with the promise of more as they needed them.

The entire family was shocked and pleased at the same time. For a few minutes, it seemed as if they thought we were crazy. There was a lot of furtive whispering among the children and a few "No, you didn't" murmurs among the adults. Whatever it takes.

A few weeks later, Kelly returned to the scene with her special red velvet cake. This time, when she arrived, she found Great-Grandma sitting in a chair on the porch with all the Red Cedar–age children gathered around her as she read to them, beaming in Kelly's direction.

It seemed as though the desserts had opened a door—the door to trust. The personal "sweet" touch was perceived by the matriarch as a sign of goodwill on the part of the school, enhancing our credibility. She became far more open to communicating with the teachers and helping the children in her household with their homework. One time, she even called Kelly for help in understanding one of the children's assignments. We had never received a call from anyone in that family for anything like that in the past. In short, we were becoming a team.

But this kind of teamwork is like a subscription service. We needed to keep paying (with our attention) to make it a success. So even though it was rare for any of the women in the Mayweather family to be at school, when one of them did come, usually at dismissal time, Kelly and I were on the lookout for her and made it a point to ask if there was anything she needed. We're both there anyway, supervising the students boarding their cars for the ride home, so it's an easy thing to do. Kelly, in particular, does a great job keeping tabs on parents at that time of day. It's a super vehicle (pun intended) for keeping the lines of communication open.

Is all this a bit too much to ask of us? Yes, it is. But we do it anyway. It's what we do. I learned a long time ago that anything any of us can do to facilitate positive relationships is time well spent. It gets the teachers and families rowing the boat in the same direction.

Months later, the Mayweather children's grandmother came to school just before dismissal. I was in the parking lot and noticed her demeanor. She was fuming. Apparently there was an issue with immunization records. We had mailed notices to the family that seemed to have been overlooked, and Nurse Byrne had just called the Mayweather home to say that in another three days, one of the children would be excluded from school until we either had proof of immunization from a doctor's office or an approved request for exemption provided by the South Carolina Department of Health and Environmental Control. This is the law in our state.

Let's take a beat here. You know the feeling you get when you go to the department of motor vehicles and find out that you've been standing in the wrong line for forty-five minutes? Well, that's where Gram was at that moment, times ten. "What in the world is this foolishness?" she asked. Remember her mother's statement, "I don't play"? This woman was not playing. The grandchild in question had just begun living with the group, and Gram had "no idea if she's had her shots, and you're going to send her home if she doesn't get them? What in the world!" A satisfactory and peaceful resolution to this challenge seemed a tall ask.

But after Kelly's work with the family, and because Gram and I went way back, I could calm her down. Her daughter had been a student of ours at Bluffton Elementary School. Gram knew I had cared for her daughter when she was a young girl.

I asked Gram, "Do you trust us to work with you to solve the problem?"

Gram's face did not change initially. "I don't know," she said. "I don't know about these shots. And I have nothing to say to that nurse who called."

I told her I understood and that I was sure we could work it out.

Gram then talked quietly about how hard it is to get everyone to do what they should be doing in the household, and this added issue was not helping matters. I asked Kelly and Nurse Byrne to join us on the blacktop, assuring Gram that Nurse Byrne was not the devil incarnate and we could work this out among us. Nurse Byrne added some things to the conversation that she never got to say on the phone—important things, such as the fact that she would be happy to call the doctor's office where the grandchild had, indeed, received her immunizations. That made it all work.

"So are we good, Ms. Mayweather?" she asked.

Gram glanced at me, half smiled, then looked at her shoes. "Yeah. We good."

I was going to offer the old standby "Before you get angry next time, just call and talk to Kelly or me," but enough was probably enough for one day.

Then and Now

It might seem unbelievable to some people that a couple of desserts could go such a long way in bringing about change in the Mayweather family. But it wasn't the desserts themselves—it was what they symbolized.

The Mayweather children's grandmother and great-grandmother likely went to school in an age when parents and grandparents had very little to do with schools. It just wasn't the way it worked for low-income folks in the South during those days. They sent their children to school, but anything more than that was too much to ask.

Back then, children sank or swam in school. There was little help coming from the teachers. In some places, parents offered little assistance too. That's what these women experienced—and worse, if they attended a recently integrated school in the South. So now that they're grandmothers and great-grandmothers, if they feel unseen and unheard by their own families, and if they feel as though they are being treated the same way by us, then they're surely not going to rush to comply with school rules, and we're not going to get very far in our partnerships with them.

Thinking that the two senior women in the Mayweather household were going to do what we needed them to do was highly optimistic. We needed an extraordinary show of outreach to this family, something that said, "We see you; we hear you; we're here to help you." At Red Cedar, we need to build trust with the people who step in suddenly to raise housefuls of children. That's what highly effective schools that serve traditionally underperforming students do.

Food is an issue. Clothing is an issue. School supplies? We give them to the Mayweathers and many other families, thanks to donations from churches. One day this family was two hours late for school because the kindergartner couldn't find her shoe. No, she didn't have another pair. After we asked what caused the problem, Great-Grandma said that they had to take up all the air mattresses on the floor to find that shoe.

Oh—and that reminds me. We need to get those folks some beds.

"We Can Do Anything!"

Another aspect of our unique school culture at Red Cedar is the Foxes Rock Drum and Dance Team (see pages 40, 71, and 102). Before every team performance, whether in a parade or a concert, I pose one question to the students: "Can we do this?" And the team supplies the answer: "We can do *anything*!"

This highly energized exchange, said with such pride, cuts right through me every single time. It's amazing and gratifying.

I started my first drum-and-flag team at Heritage Elementary School in Lynchburg, Virginia, where I held my first job as a school principal. Robert, the director of the band at Heritage High School, located just down the hill from our little elementary school, was thrilled because my team would help generate excitement for his band when the students grew up. Team members had a head start on handling drumsticks and flags and felt like they knew what they were doing.

Robert once invited our ragtag little group to perform at a football game. We fared pretty well for a band of drummers, flag bearers, and bell players who were only in their second year of playing their instruments. And we received a spectacular and generous ovation from the crowd. Those children had to feel like they were on top of the world!

Yet I doubt anyone could have felt as proud as a ten-year-old named Louis did. Louis was a tough fifth grader whose mom was largely absent from his day-to-day life. I was thrilled and surprised that she got him there to perform on the snare drum with us.

At the close of our event, we marched toward the home-team stands, where the cheering was still going strong. We stacked up our lines near the fence that separated the fans in the stands from the track and the field and made our way toward the exit gate. It was there where the families would reunite with the performers.

Amid the cheers, I kept hearing from the sidelines, "That's my son! That. Is. My. Son!" I followed the sound and saw Louis's mom standing at the fence. Her head went back and forth: first she would look at Louis, then she'd look back at the crowd. Chills.

Our culture at Heritage Elementary was built around the word *pride*, and that moment exemplified it. For some children, we offered a team they could belong to, a team parents could feel good about supporting. For other children, we had different ways to help them feel as though they were part of something bigger than themselves. We worked to find something compelling for all students. They needed a reason to come to school each day, and we tried to give them one.

It's the Little Things

Besides offering students the opportunity to join a one-of-a-kind drum-and-flag team, we do other practical things at Red Cedar to create and maintain our school culture. For example, classical music—or, at times, jazz—is always playing in our hallways. It promotes a certain peaceful, respectful, refined attitude as students and teachers go about their day. Classical music was my first choice because it inspires the demeanor we would like our children to adopt.

In addition, some students might not have as much exposure to classical music as they do to other genres. I recommend that any principal who has the opportunity to help build, outfit, or rehab a school secure the wiring, speakers, and production equipment necessary to send music throughout the building.

School culture is powerful. It's the driver of everything else that happens around it. Big things, little things—it all matters.

One not-so-little thing is the way adults interact with the students in the building. As many staff as possible are in the hallways, outside, or in the cafeteria to say hello, especially when the students come in the door in the morning. We want to fill as many buckets as possible as soon as our students make it on the property, especially the ones whose buckets are closer to empty than full. For them, a positive school culture is less a nicety than a necessity.

A Great Idea That Evolved into Something Even Better

Have you ever seen a book vending machine? It's exactly what it sounds like. The one at Red Cedar was customized for us with a vinyl wrap that bears our name and school colors. It also features a FOXY APPROVED insignia emblazoned on its side, a nod to our beloved mascot. It is loaded with a great variety of top-quality books chosen by our assistant principal, who found an anonymous donor to fund it. It's yet another example of the ways we create a school culture that encourages optimal learning.

How it works: a student peruses the selection of books in the machine, deposits a token to "purchase" the book, punches in the number of the book selection, and voilà, the book drops down, just as if it were a bag of Doritos or a Snickers bar. But it's a book.

If you think about it, reading a book is like time traveling. Children can go anywhere within the pages of the story. It's also a tangible gift they can keep forever in their home libraries. In short, a book is an amazing acquisition on its own, but there's an additional magic when it's delivered by a machine. And it's that magical aspect that fits our school culture. "But wait; there's more!" as they say on those "only on TV" commercials.

We had no idea how we would award the tokens that the children deposit in the vending machine. That is, what does a student need to do to earn one and receive a book? Conveniently, around the time the machine arrived, the state test scores from the previous year had been released, and we had four students with perfect scores on the math portion of that exam. One of the teachers of our gifted and talented students, who is also the leader of the Red Cedar "chapter" of the Get Your Teach On team,[46] suggested that these four math geniuses be the first recipients of the tokens. It was a brilliant idea. Our district superintendent, Dr. Rodriguez, came to christen the machine and award the tokens.

Soon after, with all the students buzzing about the tokens, I heard a story from our behavior management specialist that had been relayed to him by one of our bus drivers. A third grader named Jelani was quietly attempting to deescalate an argument between his cousin and two other boys on the bus one day. Eventually, he got them to sit down together and put aside the idea of a physical fight. He reminded them that they

[46] Get Your Teach On is an organization that "specializes in professional development and encouragement for educators and administrators in the form of conferences, workshops, and events." See https://www.getyourteachon.com.

would get in trouble if they continued doing what they were doing. Mr. Rod told me, "I don't know what gets somebody a token, but that was pretty awesome." The next day, I related the story to the students and staff on the morning announcements and saved the mention of who was responsible until the end.

When I did, I said, "So Jelani is going to come down the hallway from his classroom shortly to meet me and get a coin for the book vending machine. As he does, if you're nearby and want to congratulate him, consider stepping out into the hallway to make that happen, because he deserves it."

The applause was heard throughout the corridors. Our hero's photo was taken, and a narrative of his accomplishment was posted on all our social media accounts. It was extremely well received, so he was further validated with many positive comments. A quiet third grader, just doing what he thought was right, became a hero with a little help from us.

Think back to your eight-year-old self. What do you think an announcement to your classmates about your good deed and a subsequent walk of pride would do for your outlook on life?

The next day, a third grader named Felicia approached her teacher, asking, "Can I nominate someone for one of those Jelani coins?" She not only wanted her friend acknowledged for something wonderful but also named the coins after their first recipient.

Felicia's teacher asked whom the girl wanted to nominate and why. Felicia explained that the previous week, her bicycle had gotten a flat tire as she was riding home from school. A boy in her class named Peter was passing by and stopped to help her. He suggested that she ride his bike while he pushed hers home. That kind of gallant kindness was worthy of a token and a celebration—very much a Red Cedar thing to do.

Red Cedar 101

Another aspect of creating a positive school culture is cultivating our relationships with parents. So during the first few weeks of school, we offer an orientation program to help them understand both our curriculum and all the recreational programs we offer. In addition, and far more important, we brief parents on our expectations, both for the students and the parents themselves. It's the Red Cedar way.

A lot of our expectations have to do with following the rules. If it's in our handbook, we will enforce it. If something in the handbook becomes out of date, instead of ignoring it, we will remove it. Questions? Call us. Expect an answer that day and a resolution very shortly thereafter. We are problem solvers, and we encourage that same behavior in our students.

At the orientation, we also explain the services provided by our counselor and social worker. Understandably, some parents hear the words *social worker* and interpret it as "department of social services, here to scrutinize my parenting."

Of course, the departments of social services in every state have an extremely difficult and necessary job—protecting children from harm and threats of harm, often in their own homes. But for our purposes, a distinction must be made between what they do and what our school social worker does.

The latter connects parents with services they might not know exist and works hard to ensure our students' welfare. It's a colossal task. It is also continually shifting in the wake of societal changes. Both our counselor and our social worker try very hard to help students and parents understand that they are there to address needs—everything from just plain listening to serving as a clearinghouse for information about the physical, emotional, and psychological support systems that are available to them.

Handle with Care

Teachers depend on parents to tell them when something traumatic happens at home because such an event can directly affect a child's emotional state and performance in the classroom. Sometimes, though, that might not be "top of mind" for parents. But it works out better when we are aware of whatever happened.

For example, a bright-eyed five-year-old named Jonathan came to class one day with tears running down his face. After some quiet coaxing, we discovered that his dog had disappeared from the house. And the pet could not be found.

That same day, Jonathan's well-meaning kindergarten teacher was set to read aloud to the class a book titled *Can I Be Your Dog?* It's about a homeless pup named Arfy who sends letters to every house on Butternut Street, pleading with the families there to adopt him.

To avoid what would have been a disastrous addition to an already terrible morning for Jonathan, the teacher scrapped that idea fast. She read another book and relayed the information about the missing dog and its effect on the boy to our social worker, who observed him to determine whether he might want to have a chat about it. She also touched base with Jonathan's mother to ask if she had any thoughts on ways we could or should support him through his loss.

We encourage parents to communicate key family events to us *before* their children arrive at school. After all, we can't know what has befallen a family unless they tell us about it. And in this case, of course, Jonathan's family would have no way of knowing we were scheduled to read a book about a dog that day. You could call this a "handle with care" approach.

Of course, there are exceptions. Sometimes events at home cannot and should not be shared with us. That's fine. Just tell us that the child is likely going to have a rough day so we can, yes, handle him or her with more care than usual. Communication is key if we are to support families.

You're Going to Write about Branding, Aren't You?

Dr. Candace Bruder is the communications officer in the Beaufort County School District, and she knows a thing or two about communicating in ways the public understands. Someone once said that a diplomat is a person who can tell you to go to hell in such a way that you will look forward to the trip. That's Candace. And she told me that if I was going to write a book, I absolutely had to discuss branding.

Branding has been considered the central nervous system of selling since the times when people traded animal pelts for sacks of flour. It assures that customers recognize one seller's products over all the rest—as goods or services whose quality is assured and sold by people they know, like, and trust. That's branding. Even though branding does not have the same long history in public schools as it does in sales and marketing, it should be one of a school administrator's top considerations.

Picture an old woman leaning on her cane. Imagine that woman shaking her finger at a small group of young principals, offering a warning: "Someday, who knows when, three students will get sick on some spoiled milk at your school. If you have never paid attention to branding—to marketing your school with intentionality—years from now, when your school's name is mentioned, some people will say, 'Isn't that the spoiled-milk school?'" Now lose the cane in your mind's eye, and you'll see me talking to anyone who ought to listen.

Intentionality is the important thing here because if you don't feel passionate about your school—the culture and the climate it creates—you have very little to brand. I used to joke with my great friend Larry, whom I met through my years here in Beaufort County, about the average quality (on a good day) of one of our former bus transportation providers. Larry was particularly frustrated with the company one morning after having learned that a series of boneheaded decisions resulted in substantially more delays and missed student pickups than usual. My response was to pose this question: "Do you think that when the team from the Beaufort chapter of this national company meets up at the annual convention with other chapters from around the country, they cheer, 'We're number twelve! We're number twelve!'" It still cracks us up every time. (It takes very little, obviously, for us to summon a laugh together.)

My point is that as a team begins to discuss the branding of anything, they darn well better have something to brand. That bus company would find a branding exercise less than pleasant because they would be bereft of any shiny objects to point to with pride. What to do in that case? Do better. Ask yourself, What do you want to be good at, bus company? What do you want to be good at, little elementary school? Then do that. And be very good at it. Talk about it. Write about it. Improve on it. Brand it.

A positive school culture doesn't happen by accident. It doesn't develop overnight, but it is easier to maintain than to build from scratch. Begin by establishing relationships with key stakeholders and identifying your mission and values. Consider the rules, norms, lifestyles, and traditions of the school. Take branding into account. With a positive school culture, your organization becomes a life-giving, model-student-creating environment where no upset kindergartner's cry goes unheard and young people are permanently influenced for the better.

CHAPTER 10

Angels in the Classroom

A Love Letter to Teachers

AS A LONGTIME SCHOOL PRINCIPAL, I'M OFTEN ASKED, "What makes a great teacher?"

Having interviewed and hired hundreds of teachers over a period of thirty years, I've thought about this a lot. So there are some traits that instantly come to mind.

First and foremost, great teachers have highly developed communication skills and an engaging classroom presence. They're able to expertly impart information in a palatable way. If you visit their classrooms, you'll notice them modulating their voices and physicality in order to effectively capture the attention of the group. They're great at improvisation and can make any lesson logical, fascinating, and at times even entertaining.

While exceedingly articulate, such teachers are equally good at listening to students, understanding their needs and perceptions. They're highly intuitive and expertly able to "read the room" and detect emotional and mood changes in their pupils. This ability is key since so many students are dealing with steep challenges at home or within their own minds. Doubts and insecurities can do a number on a child's self-esteem. As one such insightful teacher, José Vilson, says, "Most of my work as a math teacher isn't even math. It's helping students believe that they can also do math. We don't talk about that enough."

In addition, while teachers must express empathy and treat students compassionately, they also have to firmly maintain high standards for behavior and academic expectations in the classroom. It's a balancing act, and experienced teachers have mastered it.

All in all, teachers have a huge responsibility in taking care of our children, which is why I wanted this chapter to be a love letter to them, capturing my respect and admiration for them.

A Heavenly Choir

In 2022, several of our teachers shared with me some of the most treasured compliments they received from students, former students, parents, and colleagues. While some compliments from students are general ("I love you"; "You always smile"; "You make me laugh"; "You're nice") and some compliments from parents are equally general ("I don't know how you do it"; "Thank you for caring for my child and helping her grow"; "You're amazing"), many more are specific and speak to what we look for in the teachers we want to join our team. For example, this comment came from a mom at the end of the school year to a second-grade teacher: "Thank you for all your communication, your support, your help, and what you have taught our daughter. You are so very supportive, encouraging, and inspiring." That parent also appreciated the teacher's help with a medical issue the child was just learning how to handle.

Being supportive, encouraging, and inspiring are critical qualities for teachers and other school staff members. They need to convince all students that they can do difficult things and do them well. The mantra for all humans throughout the school must be "You can do anything."

When adults and children alike begin to believe it, they start looking for the next challenge.

Most of our teachers "loop" with their students as they move on to the next grade level. For example, third-grade teachers teach the same group of students they taught in second grade; fifth-grade teachers teach the same group of students they taught in fourth grade. This is done to establish continuity and help cement the close relationships between students and teachers that form throughout the year. Teaching students for two years rather than one means that a teacher's impact on those students is stronger. Classroom communities are tighter. And empathy and a sense of community are greater among the students and teachers.

Following are a few examples of teachers who have made huge differences in the lives of their students—a choir of angels, if you will.

Dee

Dee loops from second to third grade. At the end of one third-grade loop, a student of hers named Ian, known to all of us as much for his wit, logical reasoning, and reluctance to be pushed as for his unique challenges, made an equally unique observation about his teacher. He said to her, "You are the nicest mean teacher ever!"

There's a lot in Ian's statement about who Dee is—or at least who Ian thinks she is. She sets high standards and expects him and his classmates to reach them. That's the "mean" part—not letting students give anything less than their best effort. She is patient and empathetic on the road to student success because almost never do all students comprehend a given lesson the first time it is presented. The teacher then must shift gears to make the material more digestible, back up and review it, teach bits of it via small-group instruction, scaffold what students know to what they do not know, and pursue any of fifteen other options. Ian also knew on some level that Dee exercised a fair degree of patience without lowering her standards whenever he pushed back against her demands that he increase his efforts to meet them.

There's a phrase for the way Dee, and so many other teachers like her, handle their business. She is a *warm demander*.[47] She attempts to convey a positive, supportive feeling toward her students while insisting that they demonstrate their best efforts and exercise self-discipline in order to achieve at the highest levels possible. Dee is just one example of this manner of teaching. So many of our teachers, and others with whom I have worked in the past, especially those who teach second grade or higher, display genuine affection toward their students while expecting nothing less than their best work.

The most talented teachers know their students, know their subjects, and know how to teach them. This does not mean teaching every fourth-grade math student every aspect of mathematics at a fourth-grade level. It is simply impossible for every fourth grader to be at fourth-grade level in every facet of a given subject area. Therefore, the best teachers differentiate their instruction to meet each child at his or her level of understanding and ability to demonstrate it. That is one ingredient in the secret sauce of fine teaching. The other ingredient is truly caring about students. This leads teachers to do whatever they need to do to be the best they can be—including but not limited to participating in workshops, taking graduate courses, consulting with specialists regarding individual challenges, collaborating with team members, and participating fully in weekly professional learning community activities.

Kristen

The following story about Kristen illustrates what a great teacher looks like. Her combination of skills and personality characteristics is somewhat rare in the general population of teachers but is not uncommon among the many teachers with whom I've had the privilege to work.

---

47 The phrase comes from Zaretta Hammond, *Culturally Responsive Teaching and the Brain: Promoting Authentic Engagement and Rigor among Culturally and Linguistically Diverse Students* (Thousand Oaks, CA: Corwin, 2015).

I met Kristen when she was assigned to Bluffton Elementary School for her student teaching during the time I was the principal there. From the earliest stages, and atypically for someone so young, Kristen had a good grasp of what it takes to be a fine teacher. She understood, with the help of her supervisors and mentors, that teaching is a craft that requires an open mind, the ability to be coached, a desire to be the best, and the will to continually improve. Creating joy and magic is optional but tends to be a by-product if all the above are firmly in place.

We hired Kristen as soon as she finished her student teaching—she was too good to lose. When I became the first principal of Red Cedar Elementary School in 2009, she followed me there, as did several others at Bluffton Elementary. Kristen has spent most of her career teaching the littles in kindergarten and first grade, with a short stint in second and third grade at my request. She's a team leader and has been for most of the time she's been a teacher. Kristen has also shown her ability and desire to lead by working with student teachers. She is patient and thoughtful with her mentees, and most important, in my opinion, she shares her passion for the vocation of teaching with them. She works to instill a love of learning—reading in particular—in her students as well.

Like many teachers, Kristen has had a side hustle from time to time in order to help make ends meet. Since we live in a resort-adjacent community—Bluffton being the last piece of real estate tourists encounter before they enjoy the beaches, golf courses, and adult beverages of Hilton Head Island—some teachers work for the condo rental agencies in the area that supervise the cleaning and maintenance of Hilton Head's visitor accommodations. Not incidentally, Kristen and her husband have four children, the oldest of whom is in sixth grade. The family leads an active life, with Scouts and camping and Disney and clubs at school along with activities associated with their extended families, also here in the area.

Kristen takes graduate-level classes and wholeheartedly participates in school-based professional development to keep current in areas where she believes she can use more support. I mention those facts lest you forget that teachers have lives to live: bills to pay, laundry to do, gutters to clean, and children to spend quality time with each night. Some educators have to carefully plan their day-to-day routines so that their work lives and professional lives stay in balance.

I recently asked Kristen to fill in the blank in the following statement, "I've been a teacher now for a while, and I'd just like people to be aware of _____."

The following is her reply:

> I think about my students all the time, even when I'm not in the
> building. I work almost every night after my own children go to
> bed to get everything ready for the following day. I am constantly
> on a search for the next great book so I can ignite a passion for
> reading in my students. I am a lifelong learner and continue to
> hone my craft, even after eighteen years. I work really hard to
> help all my students feel special and loved. They are 100 percent
> free to be themselves in my room.

You might think this is the approach all teachers should take to their profession—this or something similar. If so, I agree. And through a confluence of the efforts of many within our school and throughout our school community, this is the profile of a Red Cedar Elementary School teacher.

Can teachers like Kristen be found outside the walls of our school? Absolutely. And when you find one, I suggest you do all you can to encourage and reward him or her. The many fine teachers I have known would do just about anything for their students, including some things I will never hear about even though I might be or have been their principal. They pray for their students, they cry about them, they conceive of new and innovative ways to teach them, and they feel most successful when their students grow.

The best, most effective teachers I've known put their everything into their teaching. But most of them believe that the general public, save for some very dialed-in parents and their former students, do not understand or appreciate the lengths to which they go in order to thoroughly teach their students the curriculum while attempting to create magic in the process.

Kristen is exceptional at what she does. I profiled her because she represents so many incredible educators with whom I have worked. They are angels. Full stop.

January

January has taught littles with us for three years now. Her answer to my fill-in-the-blank question was the following:

> Before I worked in a school, I had no idea that teachers prepare lesson plans every night. I did not know that teachers go to sleep thinking about that student who is constantly interrupting the mini lesson or complaining, trying to figure out how it can go better the next day. I did not know that I would be fixing things like broken hearts and empty bellies before I could teach the lessons each morning. I had no idea that some parents do not care or are just too overwhelmed by their everyday lives to be able to work with their kids on sight words. I want people to be aware that teachers want to be on your team. We want to collaborate on your child's needs and celebrate their successes together.

January's concerns about the challenges her students bring with them to school are very real. The issue is complicated by the fact that a portion of the population doesn't believe that those challenges exist. And some people who do believe it have an expectation that schools can overcome those challenges on a student's behalf.

In addition, some of the students who have the greatest challenges have parents who don't want us to know about them. It makes for a complicated chess match.

Part of what teachers do in their jobs is dictated by law. For example, if we believe that a child is being abused or neglected, it is our obligation to report it to the department of social services and sometimes to the police. All concerns require our attention and appropriate responses and receive exactly that from a whole team of individuals, starting with the classroom teacher. Our students need to feel that school is a safe place and, second, a happy one.

Can't We Just Take Them All Home with Us?

In Lynchburg, a gentleman named Bob Dozier worked as a liaison between the schools and the business community. His goal was to help form partnerships between education and commerce so that students could reap a wide range of benefits, not the least of which were opportunities to apprentice at local businesses. To help the partners he was recruiting relate to day-to-day life in the classroom, Bob used the analogy of an automobile factory.

He'd tell the members of the Rotary Club or the chamber of commerce that at a factory that turns out SUVs, when the lights go out and the conveyor belt stops at the end of the day, everything stands still, and security is in place. Nothing moves, and nothing changes overnight. When the assembly-line workers come back in the morning, they find every unit just as they had left it the previous evening, waiting for the next step in the process to begin.

In schools, however, our "units" go home every night. Some of them return to school stronger, wiser, and happier than they were the day before, ready to learn. Maybe they completed a project with Dad yesterday after school and even have a great video of it to proudly show their teachers. Maybe Mom spent double the amount of time she usually spends reading to them, and that sent them off to dreamland as content as can be.

Or maybe—and I know of far too many of these situations—something awful happened during the night that the child witnessed. Maybe it involved violence, the consequences of drug use, alcoholism, sexual abuse, or neglect. Bob would say, "You see, ladies and gentlemen, everything you're working on stays safe all night. Whatever state of completion it's in, it's going to stay in that place. The next day, or whenever you turn the lights back on, you pick up where you left off. But some teachers can't start where they ended with the children because they must first repair the damage that was caused the previous night—or at least try to do so. In an automobile factory, that's like having to back up the assembly line every morning so you can replace a dented fender here or a flat tire there. That will slow down the whole process."

Beyond that, Mr. Dozier, some dents are so deep that the superficial repairs teachers can perform might make things *seem* all right, but the hidden damage could be left unaddressed for a very long time. And in our little "cars," dents are not always visible, nor are the cars always able to verbalize what happened to cause them. Likely they were told not to share such details.

Remember the "Maslow before Bloom" concept—the idea that we cannot expect children to fully engage in learning when their basic needs are not met? That's what teachers confront. The best teachers know their students well and can sense when something is not quite right at home. They are willing and able to find the resources to address a child's basic needs. They will do whatever it takes. But sometimes, despite our best efforts, the solutions are beyond us. More than once, usually late in the day, I have heard it said (or I have said myself), "If we could just take them all home with us." We want to help and can hardly bear it when we cannot effect the changes that could improve the course of a student's life. But we rally and come back the next day, and we keep on trying.

What Teaching Is Really Like

"I thought I knew, but I had no idea." That's what a second-year teacher once said to me when I asked if she had known what to expect during her first year of teaching. She didn't anticipate being challenged by her students and their parents over important things and trivial things alike. She didn't know she would be susceptible in her first year of teaching to every childhood disease, including many she had not experienced in her own childhood. (Full disclosure: I had actually hoped to acquire measles, rubella, and strep throat when I was a student teacher so I could get them out of the way before I was hired. By "happy accident," I did indeed contract them all, though they were not the joyful experiences this expression implies.) The young teacher went on to say that she also did not foresee how difficult it would be to confront so many different levels and kinds of student needs.

If you are over the age of fifty or so, and you attended a typical public school, the chances are very good that your classmates were like you in most any way you might imagine, including prior academic achievement, family income, native language, and maybe race. That is no longer the case and has not been for quite some time. In bygone days, students with significant special needs were often sent to off-site programs that took them away from their "home schools." If they had a learning disability, it was likely not diagnosed. If it was diagnosed, it was not really addressed. If the issues were somewhat mild, they attended school with the rest of us, and schools dealt with those challenges (or not) as they chose.

That's also how things worked for students whose first language was not English. And that was status quo for students with emotional and behavioral issues. If their challenges were so daunting that they could not function in "gen ed," as we call it now, there were special schools for them to attend, but those placements were apt to isolate them from their peers. This deprived them of the opportunity to be exposed to challenging material and the chance to acquire and practice the age-appropriate social and life skills important to all children's development.

Laws, best practices, and teachers' skill sets have changed over time—decidedly for the better—and now address the needs of students who fit these descriptions. It wasn't that the young teacher who didn't know how difficult it would be to meet the needs of all her students was ill prepared; there was nothing wrong with her degree and certification program. Her undergraduate coursework was more than adequate. She took special education classes and those that would prepare her to teach students who speak little to no English and cannot read in their native language. She would also have learned how to assist students who have experienced trauma. And she is not complaining that she is expected to teach students in the way they best learn or that she must meet them where they are both academically and emotionally.

Rather, her point was that in a class of around eighteen students, likely four or five of them are in one of these categories. And they are almost never in the same place on their journey. What she is saying is that she needs to personalize the lessons for many if not most of them. That means she is serially adapting her delivery of instruction based on a continuous feedback loop provided by formal and informal assessments of her students' understanding of the material she presents.

Before we knew better, as teachers, we would have just pushed onward through the lesson regardless of whether all the students actually "picked up what we were putting down." In some cases, back in the day (and now in less-than-exemplary classrooms), a teacher might not even realize exactly what each student does and does not know. That's unacceptable now. To paraphrase Maya Angelou: before, we did what we knew how to do; now that we know better, we do better.

Parents Who Help—and, Well, the Others

There are parents who make lunches for the entire team of fifth-grade teachers in our building. That could be because they have an extremely high level of respect for the teachers' equally high level of commitment to their students. Or it could be some sort of admission of and subsequent compensation for sending challenging-to-teach offspring to school every day. Or perhaps the teachers have mounted a brilliant marketing campaign targeted at the parents. (Take my word for it: they are quite capable of such voodoo, which means that their lunch-acquisition game is just as on point as their teaching chops.)

That's an extraordinary example right there, but other parent-generated gestures are just as supportive and heartfelt. There are parents who make tamales and bring them to their children's teachers. There are parents who clear the teachers' Amazon wish lists. There are parents who send kind notes or look a teacher squarely in the eye and say, "Thank you for all you do for my child. You have made an incredible difference in our lives." That last one generally means the most. That and "I don't know how you do what you do, but I'm sure glad you do it" are the gold standard of affirmations for teachers.

Parents who make these gestures are a rare breed—empathetic and thoughtful, clearly putting themselves in the position of a teacher and thinking, *Good Lord! Really? How can a person manage to do this job well?* I would like to believe that if everyone had the ability to empathize that way, there would be a lot less of what I'm about to describe. What follows is an assortment of teacher joy killers that serve as construction cones in the arena of teaching and learning.

The Child Tells Her Parents That the Teacher "Always Yells" at Her

In one instance, after a great deal of investigation and conversation with the parent and child and teacher, we concluded that when one particular child said that her teacher was "always yelling" at her, she meant that the teacher was *correcting* her.

The dad agreed with the child. "Yep, that's yelling." He said the teacher needed to stop showing the girl how to do things differently, because she really didn't like it.

Surprised and searching for clarity, I asked, "You mean that Ms. Brayshaw should not correct your child?"

Dad replied, "Yes. That's it. She doesn't like that."

I made a sports coaching analogy and eventually leveraged my way into some semblance of understanding on his part, managing to avoid saying what was on the tip of my tongue—words like *absurd* and phrases such as "Why bother sending her to school at all?" Somewhere in there, I shoehorned a question that went something like this: "So what you're saying is that unless she somehow finds her way to new knowledge outside the classroom or decides to listen to a teacher, it's OK with you if she remains in a state of arrested development that will make her a third grader forever?"

Dad said he'd think about that. Neither he nor the mom was involved much in communicating with Ms. Brayshaw after that. But we never again received pushback from them, and the child began to see that following her teacher's directions was not terrible. She even realized that it might have helped her and at times was fun. Ms. Brayshaw has her ways.

The Parents Believe the Child's Lies about What the Teacher Did, Coincidentally in Conjunction with a Misdeed the Child Committed That Is about to Come to Light

As a first grader, Lana is just learning how school works, and she is not impressed. She did not want to read the book assigned to her. After telling the tutor that she would not read that book, and after it was explained to her that she really did need to do so, she informed the tutor that she was going to go home and tell her parents that the tutor hit her. "And they will believe me," she added.

Lana was right. They did believe her. It takes a bit of time to get out of a hole like that with parents, but we did. Things are a bit better now.

The Parents Go "Mama Bear" on a Teacher before the Facts of a Situation Are Known

When a parent goes into the ultimate defend-my-child mode on a teacher, and this behavior repeats itself consistently, sometimes the parent and child fall into a rhythm of sorts. That is, one day, Mom might ask if every-thing at school that day was OK, and the child's answer is yes. That being the case, everyone carries on.

But when the child's answer is no, and Mom overreacts, the child might think that's what Mom was waiting to hear. She needs a problem to solve. There's energy behind Mom's response, and that lights up the child; maybe this is more attention than he gets for anything else. Going forward, the child is happy to oblige.

He finds a problem or slight, real or contrived, and brings it to Mom's doorstep each day. I have come to call this activity "bringing home a dead rat," much as a cat does. "Look! What do you have to say about this, Mom? Isn't this the nastiest thing you've ever seen?" Mom, quick to take up arms in a metaphorical sense, might be halfway out the door with the goal of putting the teacher's head on a stick before she even gives it much thought. Running it through her brain once more for a rationality check would be in order, but she's in battle mode now.

Being deeply involved with whatever the manufactured crisis du jour is, the parent might not realize she is being manipulated by her child and turn her anger on whoever answers the phone at the school. In these cases, we start out with one foot in a hole, but we know how to dig our way out. It takes a bit of work to break the cycle, but it can be done. You simply flip the script.

I have suggested to parents more times than I can remember that they set up a new rhythm. Going forward, they should ask their children three questions each day when they come home from school.

- Can you tell me something good that happened today?
- Can you tell me something funny that happened today?
- Can you tell me about a time when you helped someone today?

Any one of those questions might spur a quality conversation; hence, the child receives positive attention for focusing on positive things. If something unfortunate happened, he will almost certainly bring it up anyway, and we at school will address it when we learn about it.

Parent Behavior We Would Rather Live Without

In addition to the examples I've cited, there are many other species of parents that make our lives at school much more difficult than they need to be. These include:

- parents who do not sign paperwork, show up for meetings, or check their children's grades, then get annoyed when school personnel press the family to be more attentive to the children's academic life;
- parents who lie to teachers;
- parents who tell their children to lie to teachers;
- parents who put their children in compromising positions when they set the teachers up in opposition to the family; and
- parents who cannot conceive of their children having done anything wrong—ever.

All these kinds of parents make teaching more difficult. We're not trying to get "all up in your business," but when things don't make sense, and lacking straight answers to honest questions, we *will* ask more questions so that we can best serve our students. And the kind of parent who lies to us or instructs her child to lie to us *really* does not want us to ask any more questions than we absolutely must ask.

Helicopters, Snowplows, and Bulldozers

We've all heard of helicopter parents—the people who hover over their children, making sure nothing upsetting or even challenging comes their way. They do everything for their children—in the case of kindergartners, they carry them into school; at other grades they bring forgotten items to school and insist that the office folks get the computer or the lunch or the sweatshirt or the toy to class immediately; they actually do their homework for them.

Snowplow parents take matters a step further. A snowplow parent seeks to move every possible obstacle or unpleasantness out of a child's way. This includes demanding that any child with whom their child wishes to play must do so and that the school staff must legislate this situation into being. "Productive struggle"—the opportunity for students to stretch and grow and solve their own problems—is something we work toward creating in classrooms. It is strictly forbidden by these folks.

Then there are bulldozer parents. These parents bulldoze over music teachers, dance instructors, and soccer coaches—and anyone else who might stand in their way—for, respectively, not awarding their child the lead in *Annie*, though she has studied voice "since she was four"; denying their son's grandmother her one and only opportunity to see her grandson dance in a featured role; and believing that clearly Coach must have lost his mind if he plays other children ahead of their child when the others are obviously less talented.

There are more of these kinds of parents, but you get the idea. The challenges posed by parents are many and varied. But we teach children and staff members to have a growth mindset—that is, to believe in the power of *yet*, as in "I don't understand this three-step math problem *yet*." Or "I can't quite comprehend how this data set of student achievement relates to this other data set of student achievement *yet*." That's what parents should be doing for their children as well.

Maybe an addition to this group would be the gaslighter parent. This is the variety of parent who wishes for us to believe that regardless of what their child has done, there is "nothing to see here." Remember the reference made a number of chapters ago about the parent who said the knife his child brandished at a bus stop wasn't a very *big* knife? That parent was trying to talk me out of a suspension for his son—a suspension he believed would be detrimental to the boy's standing on a travel football team. His star running back had pulled the knife and verbally threatened another child, and Dad thought it would be fine for him to apologize and maybe stay in for recess, because it wasn't a very big knife. Sure, that may have sounded reasonable to him, but it certainly wouldn't help change his son's behavior for the better. (The child was suspended for three days, summoned to a hearing, and enrolled in an early offenders' program. His dad didn't see why he shouldn't play football during the days of his suspension from school. *Sigh.*)

Things Administrators Should Do to Help Teachers

Principals should continually look for ways to help teachers do their best for students. To that end, I strive to remove any construction cones that prevent them from doing that. My methods include the following.

- Respond promptly. So many times, what a teacher needs is simple. So fix it. Reply, even if it's to say that you do not yet have the answer. Then get back to them as soon as possible with what they need. This lets teachers get on with whatever is next. The boss's response or lack of it should not be what stands in the teacher's way.

- When there are disciplinary issues that involve many students at a given grade level, have a "fireside chat" or "come to Jesus" moment with all of them. This should be done with the teachers' consent and with them present, if useful, along with support staff.

- Solve problems. Most unmet needs stem from a lack of imagination. And what we do not have at Red Cedar, nor did we have at the Saltonstall, is a lack of imagination. Also remember that there are myriad sources of imagination throughout the school, not just in the principal's office. And honor that creativity when you find it.

- Back up staff members. If someone makes a mistake—missing the notice for a change in a child's transportation on a given day, for example—apologize to the parents with the teacher present. Develop a plan for preventing it from happening again, and share this plan with the parents. Follow up to see if the plan is working. After all that is over, debrief with the staff member about what went wrong. Don't participate in a meeting about a teacher unless the teacher is present. If a parent becomes disrespectful toward a teacher in such a meeting, give the parent a chance to clean that up, and if that fails, either excuse the teacher from the meeting and move to reconvene when the parent is "ready" or do the cleaning up yourself.

- Honor and respect what teachers and assistants and support staff and nurses do every day. Nothing of much importance happens in the principal's office other than making sure that what goes on in classrooms is uninterrupted and is as close to what the teacher had in mind as possible.

- Try not to deny a teacher anything that can be granted. On a macro level, Dr. Mary Stratos, the district's chief instructional services officer, does the same for principals—definitely for me. When we have an idea about a project and need permission, time, assistance, or funding, after careful questioning, we'll likely get what we need to realize that dream. Dr. Stratos understands, as do I, that even the smallest gesture of support for a teacher's flight of fancy in the name of engaging her students is golden.

- Do not tolerate chaos, drama, or inappropriate behavior.

- Keep your team in sync. When an office staff member can say to an unreasonable parent, "I'm sorry that wasn't the answer you wanted. You can certainly talk to Dr. Corley about that, but she's going to say the same thing," your team is in sync, and it needs to be that way.

- Be unpredictable on the fun side. When someone says, "What was that instrument Dr. Corley was playing at dismissal? I've never seen it before, and the kids were asking about it," you know you've created at least one enjoyable, memorable moment that day. Or when someone else asks, "Who cleaned up the goose droppings in the parking lot? I was wondering how we were going to keep that mess from getting in the building," and the answer is, "It was the principal, dressed in a Gloucester fisherman suit and wielding a power washer," you may get labeled as eccentric or a little weird, but at least you sparked a few laughs and maybe even inspired others to engage in positive shenanigans, all while keeping that nasty stuff from befouling the tile.

- Borrow teachers' brains. And don't forget to borrow the assistants' brains too. They have a wealth of knowledge and see things from various perspectives; it's definitely a lens through which administrators need to peer every now and then.
- Be funny. Be absurd. Our millennials love it when I use slightly passé superlatives such as "that's fire" and "on fleek." It humors the daylights out of them because I am so incredibly square. And who doesn't learn better when they are in a good mood!?
- Inspire teachers.
- Learn from teachers.
- Know what teachers need and find ways to acquire it.
- Learn how to make macarons.
- Grow.
- Give staff members their due, because the best of them are absolutely irreplaceable.

The finest teachers I know care deeply about their students and make it their mission to meet all their students' needs in the best way they can. What's more, when they reach their limit of time, resources, or ability to effect change, they find ways to obtain more of all those things. That's what great teachers do so well. Great teachers are angels. Really.

Epilogue

Learning and Labor

AT THE CORNER OF GREEN AND WRIGHT STREETS, THE center of campus at the University of Illinois at Urbana-Champaign, stands a bronze sculpture by Lorado Taft, cast in 1929. Weighing ten thousand pounds and standing approximately thirteen feet tall, it depicts a woman in academic robes standing in front of a throne with her arms outstretched. She is flanked by two attendants, a female and a male, who are shaking hands behind her. The sculpture's official title is *Learning and Labor*, which is also the university's motto. Predictably, the attendants in the piece are respectively named *Learning* and *Labor*. But to all who know anything about the place, this sculpture at the heart of campus is known as the Alma Mater.

The statue is the prime venue for photo ops, especially of the commencement variety.

It is iconic. It represents the university in so many ways—well beyond the T-shirts, banners, and stationery. It is beloved by many, including me. But here's the important part: there are three inscriptions on the base of the statue. One tells you who raised the money for the statue—the classes of 1923–29. Another is a Bible verse, Proverbs 31:28:

"Her children arise up and call her blessed." And the third, which appears on the front of the statue, says,

ALMA MATER
TO THY HAPPY CHILDREN OF THE FUTURE
THOSE OF THE PAST SEND GREETINGS.

From the very first time I saw it, touring the campus as a high school senior (one of those "happy children of the future"), I was taken aback by it. Stopped in my tracks. It was so powerful. Someone is trying to tell me something, I thought. Work hard. Do your best. Hone your skills.

And now that I have become "those of the past," my greetings to the happy children of the future consist of the work I've devoted my life to pursuing.

To me, those greetings, or words of wisdom, mean leading by example and leaving a legacy in concert with hundreds of dedicated educators, all driven by the desire to make valid contributions to the advancement of our craft. And I believe we have done just that. The happy children of the future, those who will take our place all too soon, will improve on what we have bequeathed to them, just as we improved on what we were given.

With intentionality, careful study, collaboration, thoughtful consideration, occasional guidance, empathy, grace, love, and a bit of magic, those children of the future will do the rocking-chair set proud. But kids, don't skimp on the magic. There's got to be magic.

Acknowledgments

ONE PERSON DESERVES ALL THE CREDIT IN THE WORLD FOR tolerating my ups and downs while I was writing this book—not to mention during the rest of the years we've been together. That singular individual is Wayne Corley, the love of my life. He casually mentioned one day that I should write a book about my life at school, then slowly ramped up the charm offensive to near insistence. Perhaps Wayne-o did not consider the impact this endeavor would have on his life. Nonetheless, he has been a trooper through the experience, as he has been in all our various adventures.

I am eternally grateful to Bob and Karla Curtis. They are among the most thoughtful, imaginative, and singularly generous people I've ever known. They, too, believed that I should write this book, reiterating that suggestion over the course of many years. They're good listeners, which is to say that when I have shared school stories, they not only asked for more but repeatedly and consistently encouraged me to write the book you now hold in your hands. Indeed, they were the driving force behind it in every conceivable way. No Bob and Karla, no book; this being among the very least of their many contributions to humanity.

Writing a first book is a daunting task. I needed a talented literary forecaddie to help me face the challenge. To that end, sincere thanks go to my collaborator, the bestselling author Glenn Plaskin. His experience, wisdom, guidance, and feedback kept me out of the ponds and most of the bunkers and made this book what it is.

My thanks also go to the dedicated team at Forefront Books, including the esteemed publisher, Jonathan Merkh, and editorial director, Jennifer Gingerich. I am grateful as well to my editor, Hope Innelli, and to copyeditor Andrew Buss.

Mary Briggs and I worked as principals together in the Beaufort County School District, and that experience developed into a deep and lasting friendship. She has always been there for me, as has her husband, Mike—never more than during the writing of this book. Mary's keen intellect and understanding of human behavior are without equal. Her willingness to help me parse what I experienced as a teacher, an assistant principal, and a principal was invaluable. To say that I deeply appreciate and admire both her and Mike still doesn't quite cover it.

I am also grateful to Cynthia Laizer, literacy coach, then assistant principal at Red Cedar Elementary School, and Kelly Wersler, the school's current academic coach, for the life we've lived together for fourteen years as work spouses. We help one another find the blessings, humor, and sadness in our experience and learn from them. I can't think of two better "wingwomen" with whom to share the ride.

All my principal colleagues and mentees have contributed to my understanding of schools and how they work, but two with whom I currently work (and debrief over an adult beverage from time to time) have a unique place in my heart: Missy Vogt and Melissa Holland. I am also grateful to Melissa Sheppard for inspiring me to really think about best practices in teaching and learning, which often leads to doing the same about life. Mona Lise Dickson falls into this category as well. Her quick mind and ability to cut to the chase, see through the nonsense, and say and do what's important in any situation continue to inform my vision.

Then there is my mentor, the late Alan Hopkins. He encouraged me to seek a doctorate. He put me on the right path in so many ways. I would be far less of an educator without his influence.

What can I say about the exceedingly quick-witted Irene Miller, my long-suffering golf partner? Yes, there's the patience she shows in tolerating my less-than-stellar play. Moreover, she has vetted many of the tales in this book (and enjoyed or feigned enjoyment of those I couldn't include here).

I have had the good fortune to work with a few very fine school superintendents over the course of my career. Topping my list and garnering my deep appreciation are Ed Curtin, who hired me in Salem, Massachusetts, and Dr. Frank Rodriguez, in Beaufort County, South Carolina. Both consistently demonstrate thoughtful, supportive leadership, with a focus on getting teachers what they need to perform magic in their classrooms. Not to be forgotten is the superintendent who hired me in Beaufort County, Herman Gaither. Then there is Alice Walton, chief administrative and human resources officer in the Beaufort County School District. Beyond having the longest title I can recall, she has talked me through ever so many dicey situations that I could easily have bungled. Much of my success as a principal might well be attributed to her wise counsel.

The Saltonstall School, in Salem, Massachusetts, provided me with a great deal of my education as an administrator. I am grateful to all the staff at the Salts for that education, especially Kris Wilson, Perla Peguero, Jane Moroney, Jane Pace, Anne LeBlanc, and Richard Stafford—my human external hard drives—who preserved memories that easily could have been lost. The whole of that group right there, and some unnamed Salts coconspirators, though always respectful to me as their direct report, taught me plenty of life lessons in Salem that proved relevant wherever I've lived.

Here's to some bonus people who have arrived in my life unexpectedly who have influenced me in positive ways. Lorene and Sarah Corley and Charlie and Sharon White are top of mind when I think of those who make my life better for knowing them.

I am grateful to every teacher with whom I have ever worked, because they and their students have taught me so much. In that vein, to my mom and dad and all the kids with whom I played endless hours of just-for-fun baseball, tennis, and some hockey at Lan-Oak Park, thank you for teaching me about fundamental fairness and how to treat people. As for my brother, Jim Klebs, who somehow pulls off a persona of equal parts protagonist and antagonist, I thank him for his forever support.